RATHER THAN REHAB

Advance Praise

"Lori Losch has written a very practical, very personal, and essential book; a step by step guide through the process of recovery, with a deep appreciation and compassion for each person's timing and profound individual differences. For anyone struggling to overcome bulimia, to master their own recovery, and their own lives, I cannot recommend this wonderful book highly enough."
— **Joel F. Wade**, Ph.D., Author of *Mastering Happiness*, Aptos, CA

"Addiction is addiction. Whether a person turns to food, drugs, alcohol, sex, gambling—or any other self-destructive behavior they can't seem to stop—it's still all about pain avoidance. In *Rather than Rehab*, Lori offers 10 strategies that will be helpful for anyone struggling to overcome the ravages of addictive behavior. As a matter of fact, these strategies are great for anyone looking to upgrade their life. You will be enriched by reading this book!"
— **Jon Butcher**, Founder of Lifebook
and Artists for Addicts, Chicago, IL

"What Lori has done, blending lessons learned on her way to recovery with what has worked repeatedly with the women she coaches, will surely illuminate the paths of may in lasting and truly transformative ways—so much so, that I am eager to share *Rather than Rehab* with colleagues who teach in Health Sciences, so that they can use it in their classes with students pursuing careers in Addictions, Health Education and Wellness."
— **Wendy L. Yost**, Distinguished Professor,
California State University, Northridge, CA

"While I haven't struggled with an eating disorder myself, I am close with people who have. *Rather than Rehab* has given me a structured way of understanding the more emotional, big-picture issues associated with the addiction of bulimia, and the freedom exercises arm me with questions to help reach out in a more supportive way than any book on the topic I have read before. Lori's honest, personal experience is woven throughout the pages, making this a must-read for anyone who wants to feel like they're not alone as they navigate the road to recovery."

— **Sara Blanchard**, Mother of two daughters and bestselling author and founder of *Flex Mom*, Denver, CO

"Upon first glance, Lori's photo is of beauty, perfection and happiness. Perfect Lori. This is an incredible story of a "Life Left of Perfect." We all have our own paths to recovery, but let her share her experience and her journey with you. In *Rather than Rehab,* she gives practical tools to start healing your relationship with food and your body. Shame seems to thrive in our secrets and Lori has so bravely shown us an alternative. It was a riveting read and I look forward to sharing it with the many people I know who are suffering!"

— **Cathie Cline**, Mother of two and Realtor, Vancouver, BC

"Addiction is an ultimate loss of freedom. It's a loss of control over your life and we are all struggling with finding our freedom. I love that Lori's book is a quest to help people regain the freedom they lost due to eating disorders. I could not imagine a better guide than her."

— **Juraj Bednár**, Founder of DIGMA, Bratislava, Slovakia

"With vulnerability, raw truth and practical, powerful tools, Lori brings the experience of bulimia out of isolation and shame, and into the heart, where we can find a path to healing, connection and freedom."

— **Jaime Myers**, Founder of Shine Life Design, Scottsdale, AZ

"Lori's courageous personal account of her struggles and ultimate triumph not only sheds light on the causes of bulimia, but she offers up useful tips on how to break the vicious cycle. I recommend this book to anyone seeking answers for any health issue because she paints the broader picture of good health and happiness, which at its heart is the ultimate union of Self with God."

— **Steve Ozanich**, Author of *The Great Pain Deception*, and the #1 Amazon bestseller *Back Pain, Permanent Healing: Understanding the Myths, Lies, and Confusion*, Warren, OH

"I was drawn to this book because of its intriguing title. I have tried it all and came to learn that recovery comes from a strong desire within as well as with being equipped with the right tools. *Rather than Rehab* is filled with practical, daily strategies. I already feel more empowered and I'm looking forward to upgrading my life by putting more of these suggestions into practice."

— **Anonymous**

"Lori Losch writes with compassion, love and the raw experience of being bulimic. She holds the reader's hand and gives practical, straightforward tools to disengage the "crazy dance" of bulimia. A must read for anyone who has bulimia or knows someone with an eating disorder."

— **Ro Rusnock**, Founder of Elements and Energy, Phoenix, AZ

"*Rather than Rehab* is a brave, deeply honest, soul-searching, poignant, and thorough examination of this dastardly addiction. Yet I love how Lori also embraced it because at a point it helped her to survive, and consequently learn and grow. This is a most powerful message for those still struggling. Other sufferers will be lucky to have Lori in their world."

— **Sandra Pais**, Mother, yogi and health advocate, Vancouver, BC

"As both a former bulimic and a wellness educator who teaches people how to partner with their body/mind, I can attest that Lori Losch has done an outstanding job of sharing the truth of what it's like to battle bulimia and win. Her recommendations, exercises, and workbook are solid support to help you lovingly shift from pain and shame to peace and partnering with your incredible true Self. Kudos to you Lori, and to every person who says yes to reading and applying this book!"

— **Kathleen Gramzay**, BCTMB, Author of
Release Your Pain, Expand Your Life! and Developer of the
Kinessage® Release Your Pain Self-Care System, Scottsdale, AZ

"Lori's personal story of suffering through, and recovery from bulimia is a compelling read and written with love and compassion for herself, and for everyone struggling with the powerful grasp of an eating disorder. *Rather than Rehab* not only gives you a glimpse into Lori's struggles and victories, it is packed with powerful insights. The Freedom Exercises throughout the book and the accompanying workbook offer tools that can be used today—practical, useful suggestions, and daily steps to help suffers take back their life, and gain control over the vicious cycle of bulimia."

— **Jo Ellen Verna**, Jo Verna Portraits, Phoenix, AZ

"I met Lori at an Eating Disorders Anonymous meeting a number of years ago and, even though she was still struggling, I knew she had the determination and wisdom to win this battle. I know that *Rather than Rehab* will help thousands recover from their eating disorders. Please trust her, read this book, and put into practice these principles. You can quit, too."

— **Anonymous**

"I'm not in recovery for an eating disorder, but many of my coaching clients are, so this book interested me. It's rare to find the level of authentic insight that Lori provides on this topic. I'm glad I picked it up because not only will it help me have more empathy for those who suffer from bulimia and to be a better coach, it has helped me see where I can even upgrade my own life! I loved it."

— **Sandra Garest**, President and
Lifestyle Coach of Lifebook, Chicago, IL

"We live in a paradox. We yearn for authentic connection & deep intimacy. We want to be seen, heard & accepted for who we truly are, yet we are terrified to truly be seen. In *Rather than Rehab*, Lori walks us through her personal journey with bulimia and addiction. Her refreshing candor and practical Freedom Exercises put the power of what's possible into the hands of those that suffer. She not only gives hope to those stuck on the merry-go-round of what feels like a never-ending cycle, she gives you the tools to embrace your inner strength and get on with the life you were born to live. This is an absolute must-read for anyone suffering through bulimia, addiction, or an eating disorder. As Lori so powerfully writes, "You are a radical truth teller given the right timing." The time is now. Tell your truth and free your soul."

— **Jenn Kaye**, Communication and Lifestyle Coach, Speaker, and Author of *Life Head-On: 6 Steps to Getting Over Yourself & On With Life*, Scottsdale, AZ

"Reading Lori's book opened me up to the many decades of self worth issues I've had over the years. Her vulnerable, real and raw stories are relatable to all women. And the practical steps she shares are enormously helpful. It's practical, real and really powerful. This book will shift your perspective, help you get out from under any disorder and change your life."

— **Steffani LeFevour**, Founder and Happiness Coach at My Happi Life, River Forest, IL

"Lori's raw exposé of her painful secret is captivating. She describes in vivid detail her own story while offering a valuable set of solutions for others. The workbook then walks you through deliberate questions, allowing you to tune into the answers you have within yourself. *Rather than Rehab* guides you down a path of self-discovery, self-acceptance, and your own achievable accomplishment. I have never had an eating disorder, yet I found the book to be helpful and relatable in other areas of my life, such as work addiction! Also, I know I will be using the smoothie recipe. It not only satiates hunger, it's delicious and HEALTHY as well!"

— **Abby Moneyhun**, Entrepreneur, Coach, and Lover of Life, Jackson, WY

"A must read for anyone struggling with an eating disorder or their loved ones seeking to better understand the harsh realities and consequences. This book dives into the truth and hardship unlike any other. Lori designed a step-by-step approach to creating a healthy life. Being in recovery myself from drugs, I understand how much work it actually takes to change your life. I guarantee the payoffs will be far greater than your wildest dreams. You've got this! Let Lori assist you in creating the life you deserve."

— **Gordie Bufton**, International Speaker, Author and Coach at Rich Legacy, Scottsdale, AZ

"In our age of social media and self-comparison, Lori's brave and honest story of her path to and through addiction could not come at a more critical time. As a mother, I am grateful for this new lens of awareness, and the empowered solutions she shares for seeing, understanding, and healing addiction. Not only will this book be a life raft to true healing for those in the painful trenches of addiction, it can help us all honor the truths hidden within us. Lori's beautiful and authentic story and voice invites us into our compassionate strength—to guide ourselves and to support each other to more healed, whole, and joyful ways of living."

— **Maria Carter**, Writer and Founder, This One Life, Austin, TX

"I'm so happy to see this information in book format! Lori was invaluable in helping me quit a brutal addiction to bulimia. It's amazing that more people will now have access to her experience and wisdom. Lori's process sure worked for me, and when I started working with her, I was hopeless."

— **Anonymous**

"I have started the 3-day challenge you suggested and it's going well so far! I am beyond grateful that you listened to my story and shared so much of yourself with me. Thank you fro walking me through this."

— **Anonymous**

"I cannot even begin to put into words how beautiful this book is. Lori is so vulnerable. Every story is tangible. I have felt the pain and lived so many similar moments. Literally. It is truly the most authentic share I have read about this very real topic, bulimia. Thank you Lori, for helping those of us who have suffered and those who may have loved ones who suffer, understand more closely the intimate details of the pain and the hope for recovery."

— **Brianna Morsa**, Founder of The Kalon Effect Holistic Exercise and Life Coaching, Gilbert, AZ

"I am seriously blown away by this book. Whether or not you have an eating disorder, all of us have some level of pain and use something to distract ourselves from that pain, whether it be clutter, social media, food, or overwork. Lori is so kind and generous and compassionate in her message; her 10 Freedom Strategies are both highly practical and deeply nourishing. Love this book!"

—**Sue Rasmussen,** Bestselling Author, *My Desk is Driving Me Crazy*, Minneapolis, MN

"The best part about this book is that it teaches you to create a set of habits and attitudes that support your happiness, and ultimately your recovery. It applies not only to eating disorder recovery, but addiction recovery in general. I loved it!"

—**Kathy Miller-Kloeber,** M.S., Health Coach, Scottsdale, AZ

RATHER THAN
REHAB

*Quit Bulimia &
Upgrade Your Life*

LORI LOSCH

NEW YORK

NASHVILLE • MELBOURNE • VANCOUVER

RATHER THAN REHAB
Quit Bulimia & Upgrade Your Life

Published in New York, New York, by Morgan James Publishing in partnership with Difference Press. Morgan James is a trademark of Morgan James, LLC. www.MorganJamesPublishing.com

The Morgan James Speakers Group can bring authors to your live event. For more information or to book an event visit The Morgan James Speakers Group at www.TheMorganJamesSpeakersGroup.com.

ISBN 978-1-68350-549-5 paperback
ISBN 978-1-68350-550-1 eBook
Library of Congress Control Number: 2017905790

Cover Design by:
Rachel Lopez
www.r2cdesign.com

Interior Design by:
Bonnie Bushman
The Whole Caboodle Graphic Design

In an effort to support local communities, raise awareness and funds, Morgan James Publishing donates a percentage of all book sales for the life of each book to Habitat for Humanity Peninsula and Greater Williamsburg.

Get involved today! Visit
www.MorganJamesBuilds.com

DEDICATION

Before I could really love you with all my heart, you loved me with all yours. You walked with me through the height of my loneliness, my crazy bulimia, and then into recovery. This book is dedicated to you, sweet Parker. You were my beloved healing talisman. Thank you for being my faithful companion for 15 years and for loving me unconditionally when I couldn't even love myself. You left Earth as I was writing this book, and my heart shattered. Though you will never again warm my bed, lick my face, or come waggling in for your morning scratch, I feel you everywhere and I'll love you forever.

TABLE OF CONTENTS

FOREWORD

"Will you show me how?" I innocently asked Diana, my uber-cool, sophisticated, teenage friend. Diana, flipped her long raven hair to one side, took her index and middle fingers, and demonstrated how she stuck them down her throat to stimulate the gag reflex. "Now you try," she encouraged. My sense of determination overruled the small voice in my heart that pleaded with me not to start what knew would be a life-altering pattern that would be nearly impossible to break. I was fifteen, self-loathing, insecure, and desperate to be thin.

In grade seven, at the age of twelve, I discovered the power of starvation, quickly dropping thirty pounds and robbing the bullies of their power. Now, three years later, I was hungry. My body was aching for nourishment and the guilt about eating was a constant companion. At fifteen, I was living on my own. My mother, a prescription drug addicted, alcoholic, seemed oblivious to my existence. My father, a man who had once been so sure of himself, had become apathetic after his second wife, my stepmother, first had an affair and then walked out on him. Left to my own devices, I sought out control and in a world where I, still very much a child, was living as an adult, bulimia became not only a mechanism of certainty, it became a dependable companion.

Initially it felt as though I had a super power. If I ate anything at all, I could trigger my gag reflex and vomit the contents of my stomach. If I was angry, upset, or depressed, I could eat whatever I wanted and then throw up. Bulimia was not only an instrument of pain management, it was also a rationalized form of self-love. It was obvious, if I loved myself, I wouldn't let myself get fat, right? Bulimia was the affectionate friend that would prevent that from happening.

It worked until it didn't. The knuckles on my right hand became bloodied and raw. People asked what happened and there were always a myriad of excuses. In the winter, I told people my skin was raw from the cold. In the summer, it was scraping my hand in some made-up task. I can't stand lying, so I was astonished at how easily the lies flowed. Excusing myself after a meal, and heading to the bathroom, any bathroom, to vomit, became commonplace. I was repulsed by my behavior, but couldn't bring myself to stop.

I found myself in a toxic relationship, which acted as a catalyst for even more toxic behavior. The binging became worse, my body began to break down, and I was put on a steroid that, in turn, ballooned my body to its heaviest weight—200 pounds. I looked in the mirror and didn't even recognize the person staring back at me. If I didn't change my self-destructive patterns, I knew I would end up dead.

At twenty years old, often vomiting blood, I made the concerted decision to claim back my life. I ended the relationship with the abusive, alcoholic boyfriend. I moved back to my hometown. I sought out reasons to love myself every day. Most importantly, I learned, over many years, how to look at food as nourishment and not as punishment. Today, I no longer binge, and haven't had the urge to purge in over thirteen years. I thank God for this miracle because, as a mother of four daughters and one son, I would not want to see my children enslaved their mother's previous addictions.

Looking back, I wish *Rather than Rehab* had existed when I was immersed in the pain of self-loathing that manifested into bulimia. Lori's personal, heart wrenching journey, and her incredible wisdom that led to the creation of this work, would surely have propelled me into faster healing in my twenties as opposed to the long, solo voyage I embarked on. I encourage you, who did not fall upon this book by accident, to come to terms with your own sorrows and make the decision to get well.

These pages, and the lessons within them, can become like the understanding friend you so desperately need if you are to heal. Every word and every exercise is provided with pure love and acceptance. Neither Lori, nor I, are here to judge you. On the contrary, we understand your pain, and the courage it takes to change your life. My wish for you is that you too will become a champion and embrace all the powerful possibilities of a life where bulimia isn't an anvil preventing you from being the amazing person you are destined to be.

— **Susan Sly**, Speaker, coach, and
bestselling author of *The Have It All Woman*

INTRODUCTION

*"Happiness is when what you think, what you say,
and what you do are all in harmony."*
—Mahatma Gandhi

It was the spring of 1995, and I was certainly not happy. My thoughts, words, and actions were so out of alignment that I was either going to check out for good or I had to check in somewhere for treatment. Once an infrequent coping skill, bulimia had become a force that consumed my life.

As with most anorexics and bulimics, I was a high-achieving addict. I excelled in school, at sports, and loved my post-college career managing a busy, hip, vibey restaurant. A close circle of friends kept me smiling, and the path to success seemed obvious and effortless. I loved my apartment in the stunning seaside community of Ambleside in West Vancouver, and life was outwardly amazing. But it was also riddled with acute anxiety. Somewhere in early childhood and beyond, I developed a sense that I was fundamentally not okay. I felt uncelebrated, misunderstood, and like I never truly fit in or was fully welcomed anywhere. I'm not saying these things were true—they were simply feelings that surfaced after a variety of hurtful experiences. We've all had them.

Insecurity arose around both my worth on this planet and my physicality. When my grandma cooed about my "spun gold hair" or random people commented on my long, lanky legs or said I will be beautiful when I grow up, it was bittersweet and brought confusion. *Am I just an ornament? Didn't you see the picture I just drew or hear the song I just played on my guitar or how kind I was to my classmate who was being bullied?* Looks seemed more important than character. And if my siblings overheard any praise, I felt guilty, ashamed, and wanted to disappear. I would think, *Please praise them too! My sister's long hair is gorgeous, and my brother's blue eyes are to die for. They are both beautiful! And talented. And smart!* I felt the extra attention became a wedge between my siblings and me that took decades to dissolve. Maybe they wanted their little sister to just bug off. Who knows? Bottom line, there wasn't that big brother or older sister love and nurture and I felt alone much of the time as a kid. Maybe we all did.

Childhood reoccurring and petrifying nightmares, moving to five different cities before the age of six, many personal betrayals, and occasional bouts of familial violence also likely helped foster a sense of insecurity and a feeling that the world was fundamentally unsafe. Fear and anxiety plagued me, but the skills to voice my feelings were absent.

With no emotional outlet, feelings became deeper and darker. Many memories throughout my childhood, teens, and early adulthood endorsed those feelings, but humans can do that. We can see only things that confirm our hunch, and we miss the rest. We can also project our fears and insecurities onto others, which only amplifies them. Rejection and abandonment, for example, can be such acute fears that we wind up actually creating them. I believe it's in the energy we emit—it attracts the same energy and becomes a self-fulfilling prophecy. It seems I did just that.

Through childhood, teenhood, and into adulthood, my anxiety increased exponentially. In the end, I couldn't cope and had to numb myself. After drugs, booze, risky behaviors, or relationships stopped working, I turned to food. As I consumed copious amounts, bulimia slowly consumed me. Binging and purging escalated from an occasional event to weekly to daily—even multiple times in a day if I had the time and enough angst to eradicate. I was also getting dangerously close to my worst nightmare: being caught. To avoid that, bulimia was a strictly private behavior. I was never one to duck into a bathroom post dinner with friends or family—that was way too risky. My acting out was always alone. Also, purging a normal-sized meal would have been too little food to produce the relief I needed. Only a major binge would do. A binge, by definition, is "a period of excessive or uncontrolled indulgence, especially in food or drink."

One such binge included a family bucket of extra crispy chicken, home-cut fries, creamy coleslaw, carrot cake with cream cheese icing, and two large diet cokes from the neighborhood KFC—I needed cheap and voluminous food in those days. I can just smell it. After driving around in my truck, likely listening to something soothing like Cat Stevens and attempting to eat away my feelings of loneliness, not enough-ness, shame, anxiety, and an overall sense that something was the matter with me, I finally pulled over to puke up the massive volume of food and liquid. I found a short dirt service enclave about 20 feet into the woods near the Cypress Park off-ramp on the Upper Levels Highway in West Vancouver and proceeded to scope out the possibilities. There weren't many.

It was dark and a bit dodgy, but I couldn't go home—my roommate was likely there. And I wasn't in the mood for yet another grimy gas station toilet. The dirt road would have to do. I opened the door, leaned out, and got rid of everything in my distended belly. Within a few minutes, I went from looking six months pregnant, to looking like a sad, starving twenty-something. But peace followed the purge. That was always the end game. Just peace.

After a short rest in the driver's seat, I was jolted out of my post binge/purge numbness by a sudden floodlight burst followed by the old familiar red and blue flashers. *S****. *F****. *S****. I shoved the wrappers strewn around into the KFC bag. But there was no missing the evidence. My shame sat in the seat next to me.

Reaching my window, the cop pointed the flashlight into my bloodshot eyes, then over to the passenger seat, then back to my eyes before asking if I was okay. This was perhaps the most embarrassing moment of my life. I was sitting in my truck just two feet above a massive pile of undigested barf. It was now an evening's snack for coyotes, bears, or any other scavengers of the night— and a hazard for the police officer's shiny black boots. He asked me to get out of the truck. It had large tires and a lift kit, so dealing with that, plus the mess below, created a less than elegant dismount.

He asked me what I was doing there.

"I'm really upset. My boyfriend just broke up with me. I'm totally sick over it," I lied without skipping a beat. What the hell was I supposed to say? That I had been driving around in yet another attempt to numb my feelings by binging on a bucket of KFC? That my roommate was home so I couldn't barf there? That this dirt enclave at the side of the highway was the only place I could find to get rid of the food I had just stuffed into my face? That sounded way too crazy. And sad.

My eyes were red. Purging multiple times will do that. So will drinking booze or smoking pot, but he didn't ask me about either. I guess they have ways of assessing these things.

After he scanned my license and registration, we stood there for a minute of awkward silence until I finally asked if he would mind if I smoked, which he didn't. I reached for my du Maurier reds and offered him one. Weird, looking back, but I guess it was just smoker's code. To my surprise, he accepted. There we stood, leaned up against the bed of my black Toyota 4x4, about five feet away from the pile of undigested food, smoking our cigarettes. We chatted easily together until our cigarettes were just filters.

When another call came through on his police radio, he made sure I was okay and then left. Before I could see the last of his taillights, I was weeping.

Later that night, I'm sure he wrote up this story with a twinge of worry. His paperwork probably went something like this:

Approached suspect's truck at Cypress Park exit.
Found large pile of vomit next to driver's side door.
Evidence of a food binge riddled passenger seat.
Suspect appeared to be sober. Sad, but sober.
No illegal activity evidenced.

I share this story to give you a glimpse into my life with bulimia. I hope you will trust me—I've been in your shoes. They may have been a different brand or style, but they were the shoes only a bulimic could wear. I know your heart. I know your pain. I know your longings. I know what you've done with food. I know what you've done to avoid food. I know your fears, at least some of them. I have them, too.

After sobbing away the feelings I had desperately tried to stuff down with a KFC family bucket, I decided then and there I couldn't live like that anymore. I just couldn't do it. I had almost been caught many times, had found myself in the most pathetic and humiliating circumstances, but none had come close to being my rock bottom as another human being having to navigate my puke pile. And, as with every addict, rock bottom is usually the turning point. I was either going to drive my truck over a cliff and be done with the pain, or I was going to check in somewhere safe. I needed a treatment center.

That decision was the beginning of a long, hard, two decade healing journey I thought would never end. Not one to readily reach out for help, I hit the library—this was long before the Internet was in every household. At the library I secretly looked for resources, careful to choose a completely private cubbyhole and to erase the search history at the end of every session. This was so embarrassing. I scoured books on bulimia, eating disorders, recovery, and rehab. I read about various healing modalities. And I searched for local treatment centers, but came up with nothing. One interesting bit of information I discovered was that according to research done by James Prochaska, Ph. D. and Carlo DiClemente, Ph. D., there are five stages to recovering from an eating disorder:

- **Precontemplation Stage**—the idea of change has not even been considered
- **Contemplative Stage**—thoughts around change are evident, but no action is taken
- **Preparation Stage**—you become determined to change, you gather resources and psych yourself up to do the work, but no real action is taken
- **Action Stage**—you actually begin to use the strategies and suggestions you have compiled
- **Maintenance Stage**—you have normalized your eating and are on the road to a full recovery.

The West Van cop experience catapulted me right into the Preparation stage.

My guess is that you are somewhere between Contemplation and Preparation. You are ready to take Action, and you are longing to live in the Maintenance Stage. Your inner self, your true essence, your soul, really does want recovery. You are tired of living a lie. Shame surrounds your secrets. Anxiety keeps you alone at night with your binge foods and the bathroom. You're tired of wiping the splattered rim for the tenth time when you should be out living life. You long for connection, but can't quite connect. You yearn for intimacy, but the thought of being truly known, seen, and heard terrifies you. And likely your most acute fear is that if you quit bulimia, you'll get fat. Yes, being fat terrifies you. Your fear feels superficial, but you wonder what will become of you if you let go of your eating disorder. Your binges are robotic, so if you stop purging, your worst nightmare will come true. You will break the scale.

Do these thoughts resonate? Does this acute fear sound familiar? Trust me when I say that though these fears seem real, they are unfounded. Fear is simply an acronym for **F**uture **E**vents **A**ppearing **R**eal. The future event of you being an out-of-control, obese person is not based in reality. I am living proof of that.

What if you could flip your thinking toward recovery from fear to excitement? What if you could alter your dialogue around your bulimia from, *screw you*, to, *thank you*? What if, for a short while during your transition from the Preparation Stage to the Maintenance Stage, you could see your eating disorder as a friend to work with rather than a foe to fight against? What if you could recognize it as an amazing survival tactic and acknowledge that it has kept you alive and comforted in this tumultuous world? Also, what if you could thank it for being a truth teller? It has shown you, in its own dysfunctional way, that you've been disconnected from your Source, from yourself, from others. What if you could be grateful that bulimia has forced you to delve deeper into yourself, your faith, your soul?

Is it finally time to step into your destiny—a life of peace, connection, hope, freedom, happiness, and love? What if your mind and your body could sense this planet is safe, you are safe, and if you release your bulimia you will be okay? Would you do it? Are you ready to quit bulimia? If your answer is yes, allow me to help. I have been where you are. I have thought your thoughts. I have felt your fear, pain, and anxiety. The details were different, but the outcome could be the same—crippling bulimia followed by a beautiful life in recovery.

FREEDOM EXERCISES

1. In your journal, record the five lowest moments you've had while acting out in your eating disorder. These can be close calls, times of deep emotional despair, the grossest places you've purged, the times you lied to people to cover up your habit, missed chances for connection, unrealized dreams—anything that comes to mind. It helps to remember the lows in order to catapult you into more highs.

2. Record the times you've been tempted to binge/purge but have chosen not to. Try to recall how you felt. Write this down.

3. Compare the two entries then spend a few minutes meditating on the second one. It might be a stretch, but try visualizing yourself embracing the possibility of living without your eating disorder.

CHAPTER 1
UNDERSTANDING BULIMIA

"What is addiction, really? It is a sign, a signal, a symptom of distress. It is a language that tells us about a plight that must be understood."
—**Alice Miller**, *The Drama of the Gifted Child*

You can't wake up every day declaring, "This is the day I will *not* binge and purge," yet fail day after day, week after week, year after year. Something has to give. Countless stories confirm this. How many addicts do you know who have overdosed? My guess is that many of these were not accidents. I can't tell you how often I longed for a heart attack. I just wanted the fight to be over, and given my system's total imbalance of sodium, potassium, and electrolytes caused by bulimia, my wish was not a pipe dream. A heart attack was a strong

1

possibility. But it never happened. So I was either going to get well or end the torment in a more sure fire way.

While suicidal thoughts plagued me, this was not an option. My mom's sweet, grief stricken face would pop into my mind, and I just couldn't do that to her. An inner knowing that there was a purpose behind my bulimia also helped me stay the course. So I set out to first understand the addictive aspects of bulimia. If I could understand why I was simply unable to quit and why normal eating seemed so out of reach, I might be able to find more effective ways to change than simply declaring my commitment verbally. I hope my research will help you on your own journey to freedom.

One of the many reasons you have been unable to quit bulimia is that it is a powerful addiction. You are not a weak-willed, gluttonous deviant—you are caught in an obsessive-compulsive and addictive cycle, and there are biological reasons for your inability to quit thus far. You are up against exceedingly powerful forces. You are neither a freak nor a hopeless case. Bulimia has been there literally to help you survive—both physically and emotionally.

There is a strong physiological cause and affect aspect that you might not have addressed, and when you begin to understand this, you can start arming yourself with more effective tools. The old "call a friend" or "go for a walk" advice when you feel a binge/purge coming on are both doable in some circumstances, but in others, your mind and body are likely screaming way too loudly. *Eat everything in sight!* In that mode, there is virtually no way out. The thought of picking up the phone, let alone actually following through with a call, is comical. Something very primal has already kicked in.

The Binge/Purge Cycle Explained

What is driving your binge/purge cycle? Why is it that no matter how many times you tell yourself, *Today will be the day,* it never is? Please go easy on yourself. Your mind, body, and soul are simply trying to keep you alive. Once you really understand these contributing factors, you will be able to take a step back, be a powerful observer, and course correct toward freedom rather than into more bondage.

There are four primary and powerful factors driving your bulimia:

1. Starvation
2. Substance Addiction
3. Behavioral Addiction
4. Pain Avoidance

Knowing there are strong forces at play will help you break down your recovery into bite sized pieces. Instead of making your goal to stop binging and purging, it might become addressing the reasons *why* you are binging and purging. Or a goal might be to create new, empowering, loving habits. Another might be to begin introducing more nutritious foods to your daily experience. This is a much more compassionate and effective approach. Rather than trying to stop your behaviors, first try to heal the underlying reasons bulimia is there in the first place.

Let's look at each factor in some detail.

Starvation

Restricting always precedes binging. It's that simple. Every living being is programed to survive—your body is constantly searching for homeostasis. It wants balance. It yearns for consistency. When it senses a famine (modern day dieting), your body will do everything in its power to ensure you get enough food for survival. And built-in survival mechanisms are much more persuasive than mental willpower. When you restrict, you will soon become obsessed with food. Powerful urges to binge will follow, especially on energy dense and sugary foods. Your appetite will become insatiable.

That absolutely happened to me. In college, I would go to school on a cup of coffee sweetened with Equal. Lunch would be another coffee and a large muffin—chocolate chip preferably. I was never into sandwiches, soups, salads, or other "normal" lunch foods. Just a muffin. Eating only that item felt empowering somehow. When I stopped eating even the muffin and survived on coffee alone, I felt even more empowered. Starving myself felt like an accomplishment. By dinnertime I was so hungry, but still only allowed myself a normal sized meal. The caloric and nutrient intake was minimal and my hipbones began to stick out. This was even more empowering. Becoming an object to be watched, rather than a person to relate with felt safe. As long as I was skinny, I was secure. Of course this was all a precursor to bulimia—my survival instinct soon kicked in with a vengeance and both binge drinking and binge eating followed by purging became my coping strategies that second year in college.

Please understand you are not a bad woman. Any malnourished person would be driven to binge. It's in your DNA. And anyone with the body image issues and perfectionism you suffer with would have to purge the binge. You began with restricting food. Your bulimia is simply trying to help you survive. Knowing this, can you have compassion on yourself? Can you even be grateful for your bulimia? It has been trying to save your life.

Substance Addiction

In the past, since food did not meet certain requirements, it was not classified as an addictive substance. However, new science has debunked this. Also, by one definition, addiction is "the state of being enslaved to a habit or practice or to something that is psychologically or physically habit-forming, as narcotics, to such an extent that its cessation causes severe trauma." Researchers rate the level of a substance's addictive qualities based on the following criteria:

- To what extent does the substance activate the brain's **dopamine** system?
- What levels of **pleasure** do users report the substance provides?
- Will a person trying the substance become easily **hooked**?
- What is the degree of **withdrawal** symptoms should a user cease using?
- How much physical or cognitive **harm** does the substance cause?

Let's look at each piece as it relates to certain foods.

Dopamine system: New research shows the same pleasure centers in your brain that light up with cocaine or heroin use, also light up after eating sugar—in fact, the nucleus accumbens lights up like a Christmas tree. This is because sugar causes dopamine, the natural "feel good" chemical in the brain, to flood the neural receptors.

The same can be said for cheese. Dr. Neal Barnard, founder of the Physicians Committee for Responsible Medicine, calls cheese "dairy crack." Why? One of the dairy proteins in cheese is casein, which breaks down into casomorphins during digestion. Dr. Barnard says, "These protein fragments can attach to the opiate receptors in your brain. As the name implies, casomorphins are casein-derived morphine-like compounds."

With continual use of these addictive foods, our brains stop producing optimal levels of dopamine, so an outside reward system becomes necessary for us to simply feel a normal sense of wellbeing. Food becomes that reward system. By binging, you are simply trying to bring your brain chemistry back into balance.

Pleasure: What isn't pleasing about sitting down to a great meal? In fact, breaking bread together has been a satisfying human ritual since the start of time. Food absolutely falls in the pleasure category. But not only for what it does to the taste buds and for social connections, it also causes a pleasing chemical reaction in your body. Similar to the dopamine effect, an increase in blood sugar levels makes you feel good. And it's not just ingesting sugar itself that does this—processed foods filled with sweeteners and refined carbohydrates such as bread, pasta, and chips have a similar affect as they all effectively turn into sugar during digestion. Your brain sees the resulting spike in glucose as a reward, so you keep wanting more. If you eat these foods often, you're unknowingly reinforcing that reward system. Eating becomes pleasing and refraining becomes painful. Food scientists even chemically exaggerate certain flavors to create irresistible taste sensations, which trigger the "bliss point"—an addictive reward pathway in the brain that keeps you going back for more.

Unfortunately, the resulting sugar surge causes your body to quickly move the glucose out of your bloodstream and into your cells for energy, so your pancreas excretes the hormone insulin to create balance. The result is a rapid change in blood sugar levels that can leave you shaky and in search of more pleasure inducing sweets, carbs, or cheese. Ham and pineapple pizza, anyone? Can you say "trifecta"?

Hooked easily: The body responds very differently to ingesting sugar or simple carbohydrates than it does to protein, fat, or complex carbs. And various people's bodies also react differently to each. Some eat sugar, feel sick, and don't want it again. Others can eat a moderate amount of it and stop effortlessly. Biologically, however, sugar does intensify food cravings and causes most people to eat more than they otherwise would. It disrupts normal food metabolism and can eventually lead to addiction.

Clearly in the case of those with eating disorders, we have been the unlucky ones who are easily hooked. Similar to the alcoholic whose one cocktail sends him into a drinking binge while his friend can have a few glasses and stop, we bulimics are prone to this sugar/

insulin cycle becoming addictive. We are similar to the alcoholic, but sugar is our vice.

Have you said, *I'll just have one bite*, when contemplating a dessert, only to find yourself licking the plate five minutes later? You were hooked easily. I'm surprised more people aren't since thousands of years of survival programing urges us to seek out highly caloric foods. We are biologically programmed to eat hyper-palatable sweet and fatty foods and our bodies are designed to store the excess calories as fat to sustain us through times of famine. It's a set up, I say! (The truth is that our DNA just hasn't caught up to the industrial age where food is often so abundant and varied—much more so than our hunter/gatherer forefathers ever enjoyed.)

Withdrawal symptoms: Abstaining from addictive foods and unhealthy eating behaviors causes withdrawal symptoms for those with and without eating disorders. Many studies have shown that completely cutting sugar from your diet leads to similar withdrawal symptoms as those experienced by drug users. A pattern of sugar binge/deprivation causes the opioid and dopamine receptors in your brain to become sensitized, leading to withdrawal symptoms such as higher levels of depression, stress, anxiety, irritability, nervousness, and mood swings.

Harm caused: According to Paul van der Velpen, head of Amsterdam's health service, "Sugar is the most dangerous and addictive substance of modern time, and more needs to be done in the interests of public health to make people aware of the many harms caused by this ubiquitous drug. The rise in obesity is also causing many other health concerns such as high cholesterol, metabolic syndrome, hypertension, sleep apnea, major depression, cardiovascular disease, diabetes, and a host of other ailments." So it does seem that sugar, sugary processed foods, and simple carbohydrates have levels of addictive qualities, based on this specified criteria, that rate fairly high.

Think back to my muffin lunches. Even the stress of college could have been the trigger that created a need to "feel better"—and sugary Mr. Muffin was right there to soothe me. Muffins became a common binge food through my 20s, 30s, and into my 40s, and still call to me loudly.

Please know you are not a freak. Sugar really is an addictive substance, and your body is likely screaming for it. You are not just a person with zero resolve, zero will power, and therefore to you, zero character. There is a biological reason you haven't been able to stop binging and purging. The good news is that biology will also play a huge role in your recovery.

Behavioral Addictions

What about the binges where you're not even using sugar, highly processed, or carby foods? What about when you just want a few nuts, but end up eating the whole bag? While your body's chemistry has played a leading role in keeping you stuck in your bulimia, there are also behavioral patterns contributing to the addiction.

According to Wikipedia, behavioral addiction "is a form of addiction that involves a compulsion to engage in a rewarding non-drug related behavior—sometimes called a natural reward—despite any negative consequences to the person's physical, mental, social, or financial well-being. A gene transcription factor known as ΔFosB has been identified as a necessary common factor involved in both behavioral and drug addictions, which are associated with the same set of neural adaptations in the reward system."

One of my behavioral addictions would kick in as I drove by certain cafes, restaurants, or food shops. I would simply deviate robotically, addictively. A totally taboo and forbidden shop under "normal" circumstances, like DQ, would yell to me as I approached. "Come in, come in! I know you want a large Cappuccino Skor Bar Blizzard®! I know you do." *Jesus. Shut the hell up. Keep driving, Lori. Don't listen!*

But inevitably, the behavioral addiction would kick in. It had become a habit. I wouldn't necessarily need a sugar high in that moment, but I just couldn't seem to fight the loud, screaming invitation. Maybe you have similar habitual behaviors? Maybe you do them out of boredom. Maybe they delay you from having to dive into a taxing project. Maybe they just titillate the rebel in you. One thing we know for sure—behavioral addiction rages with bulimia.

A phenomenon called reward sensitivity can also keep you locked into your behavioral addiction. It is a measurable personality trait that determines how driven you are toward rewarding experiences and how easily, or not, you can refrain from them. Those with higher reward sensitivity have increased activity in the brain centers implicated in eating for reward purposes. This sensitivity makes a binge much harder to resist and behavioral addiction harder to break. Years of acquiescing to the urges have created deep, habit-forming neural pathways in your brain. The good news is that the more you resist the temptations and choose recovery, the more you can reroute these pathways. But that's for later. For now, just understand that you are dealing with more than just the inability to stop binging and purging. There is a complex set of circumstances contributing to your eating disorder. But they don't have to take you out. You can absolutely create new pathways in the brain, new chemistry in the blood, and new behaviors to replace the old, destructive ones.

There is also something to be grateful for—not only has your bulimia been fulfilling a biological need, it has also been helping you survive emotionally and even grow spiritually. Deepak Chopra said, "The journey out of addiction is the deepest spiritual journey a person can take." This was certainly my experience. Even though it took me decades to get well, it was not wasted time. It was a time of deep spiritual inquiry, study, and growth. My guess is it has been the same for you. Your spirit is growing. Your soul is expanding. You are remembering who you are at your core. Try to be grateful for your bulimia. Refrain from words like, "I want to kill it, beat it, or hide it." What if you could thank bulimia for serving you? What if you embraced it as your personal survival tool?

Eventually, you will be able to say good-bye with love, but for now, acceptance and gratitude are your super powers. We all keep things until they no longer serve their purpose. That day may be today. Or it might be tomorrow. Or next week. But one thing I know, there will be a day when you look back on your eating disorder with deep gratitude. On the other side of recovery, you will be an even more empathetic, intuitive, multi-dimensional, caring person than you would have been if you had never overcome an addiction.

Pain Avoidance

Since my youth, I have acted out in one illicit behavior after another. This isn't uncommon. The statistics show that most of those suffering with bulimia have also used many other substances or behaviors. Dr. Gabor Maté, a renowned doctor in the field of addictions and author of many books, including bestseller *In the Realm of Hungry Ghosts: Close Encounters with Addiction*, says, "Addiction is simply pain avoidance."

When I look back on life, I have tried to avoid feeling pain for as long as I can remember. There were a number of traumatic childhood, teenage, and even adulthood incidents that I never processed. We all have them. Your painful experiences will be different than mine, but the point is we are all bruised bananas. And since you were probably not taught to identify, feel, and release your pain in a healthy way either, you have sought things outside yourself to ease or numb the feelings.

In the end, no pain avoidance strategies worked as well as food seemed to. Lord knows, I used many other things—cigarettes, booze, drugs, people, sex, money, success, shopping, travel, exercise—but bulimia held me tightest in its grips, trying to cocoon me from the outside world and shield me from my inner anxiety. When the emotional pain or anxiety became acute, even the *thought* of using food to numb the feelings penetrated my stress. A huge amount of mental dialogue would follow.

My Ed (short for eating disorder) was a seemingly separate voice, but was fully my own. That voice would tempt me with some food item, which my higher self would refuse. Then Ed would go on to tell me I'm useless and should be way farther along in life than I was. It would tell me I'd never find a mate to share life with—that it would always just be my dog and me. It would accuse me of being pathetic, a child. *What kind of grown woman goes into panic attacks in the grocery store?* I would fight back, but my punches would get increasingly feeble until eventually my feelings would start to spiral. I believed Ed's rhetoric and food became the only way to ease the anxiety. Inevitably, that first food item would turn into another and then another. The robotic binge would be well underway. Does this sound familiar? The dialogue may have been slightly different in each incident, but the outcome was always the same. I would give in to bulimia in order to ease the mental pain.

Once I had decided to act out, the ritual of the binge (planning, preparation, and execution) became automatic. If there was no food in the fridge, which there rarely was, the planning and preparation stage would include fantasizing about what I was going to eat then heading to a grocery store, restaurant, or fast food joint to pick up my poison. I bought enough food to feed a family. "I'm going to be the hero when I get home," would often be my comment to the checkout clerk or order taker. Looking down at the volumes of binge food was always somewhat embarrassing, so I had to let them know it was not all for me! "Can I please have four sets of chopsticks?" (or forks, straws, spoons—whatever the appropriate utensil for the food choices) was also a common cover-up line. I always wondered if they saw through the B.S. and into my pain.

Once the feeding frenzy actually started, my emotional angst would subside even further. But not totally—it was only after the subsequent purge, that my mind would finally go quiet. The purge brought peace. Every time, but never for long.

Has your bulimia been a Band-Aid for pain? I have to let you in on a little secret: it will never work. It's like trying to suture a puss infected wound. When you really understand the concept of pain avoidance, it will became clear that if you first heal the underlying pain, there will be no need for the Band-Aid of bulimia. You have been lovingly approaching it backwards—trying to take the Band-Aid off first (quitting behaviors). Ironically, that's wildly more painful than actually working through the pain in the first place. It also causes so much more shame. First acknowledge, explore, and heal the pain you've been trying to avoid, and then the behaviors will subside much more gently and successfully.

Freedom Exercises

1. Go back to your last few binge/purge episodes and ask yourself, what occurred in the hours leading up to them? Had you starved yourself? Were you craving a certain food i.e. sugar, which may indicate substance addiction? Were you acting out in a behavioral addiction? Were you in emotional pain? See if you can identify the underlying causes and triggers. Write them down. Are there consistencies? Think of a strategy you could use at the very first trigger point, and commit to implementing it the next time the same trigger arises.

2. Ask yourself what emotions your eating disorder is trying to anesthetize. See if you can step into these emotions in a healthy way. Feel them. Thank them. Share them if appropriate. Ultimately, move through them.

CHAPTER 2

EMOTIONAL HUNGER

*"There is more hunger for love and
appreciation in this world than for bread."*
—Mother Teresa

Humans have evolved to avoid death-by-starvation. The five innate internal drivers motivating us to eat are thirst, variety, low blood sugar, empty stomach hunger, and nutritional hunger. These are obviously beneficial—of course you need to keep hydrated, you need a variety of foods for their nutrients, you want to avoid low blood sugar, your stomach will give you clues as to when it's ready for more nutrition, and, if you are nutritionally deficient, you will likely crave foods containing those elements. But the sixth human hunger, and the one I find most intriguing, is emotional hunger. It seems to

13

serve no physiological need, yet it's a powerful driver. Why can ignoring emotional hunger lead to a binge? I think it's because it creates an internal void that feels insatiable, and it creates anxiety that needs medicating.

I was flipping through an old journal and the following verbatim entry screamed to me of emotional starvation and my attempt to feed it. No fault of the other people involved—it's *my* responsibility to ask for emotional needs to be met. But in my bulimic days, I was so out of tune with my needs. Even if I could identify them, I had no skills to honor or voice them.

I'm so bored with his extreme health obsession. It's dull as hell. I really don't care to be so freaking anal about it. In fact, what I have been doing all afternoon would freak the s*** out of him. This was the afternoon of my counseling session. Before session, I had invited some people over for lunch. I shopped for and prepped a lovely salad full of chicken, feta, pesto, tomatoes, pine nuts, green onions, chicken, arugula, and a gorgeous homemade dressing. They dropped in for a few minutes, but decided not to stay as they had a busy afternoon. When they left, I felt alone and not chosen. I had invited them and prepared lunch, but it seemed my company was not high on their list. Feeling rejected, I wound up eating everything I had made for them, and then some ... blueberries/ raspberries doused with almost a whole pint of kefir sprinkled with sesame seeds, granola, and topped with the homemade whipped cream I knew they liked in their coffee. When that was done, I filled up my stomach even more with gorgeous coconut water. Was so full. Had to get it out fast before my session. Quick. Purge. Purge again. Then I drank a huge glass of water, laid down on my back, gurgled it around so I could get it all out, and purged again. Always feeling like a loser freak as I washed the basin of the toilet, the seat, and made sure no other evidence remained. I am an idiot child

that can't grow up. But ... maybe there's hope ... I have Cesar in
15 minutes. Better go. As I walked down through the lobby, smiling
cheerfully at the concierge and valet guys, I felt like such a fraud.

That entry was just one day out of a thousand similar days. The spiral
was always something like either starving physically or emotionally,
feeling the pain of that, not wanting to feel the pain of that, numbing
the pain of that. So predictable. Why I was not able to say, "Hey, why
don't you just sit, and have a quick bite before going?" Or even show
them the beautiful lunch salad I made for them. But no, I just took their
first indication of not wanting to stay and gave them a quick and easy
out, no matter how bad that made me feel.

Let's explore emotional hunger more deeply so you can start to
create strategies to deal with yours.

Understanding Emotional Hunger
Eric Edmeads, Founder of *WildFit*, a global phenomenon bringing
health to hundreds of thousands of people, says emotional hunger is
driven by four core emotional needs—certainty, significance, variety,
and connection. Understanding each will help you recognize your eating
disorder's driving forces so you can quickly course correct.

Certainty
Your stress is reduced when you feel certain about your environment,
your social standing, and your food supply. Today's atmosphere of global
stress is causing many to feel uncertain, and many people deal with this
by overeating.

I definitely found that to be true. My bulimia began in college when
I was facing an uncertain future, and it escalated in my mid twenties
and throughout my life as a single woman. I wasn't certain I would find
the career of my dreams. I wasn't certain I would find the mate of my

dreams. I wasn't certain I would understand my reason for being on the planet. So much uncertainty plagued my mind, so I stuffed down the questions and purged out the answers.

Significance

Your need for personal significance is hardwired. It is important for you to feel recognized in your community because you experience less stress when your efforts are rewarded and acknowledged. Many people feel insignificant in this world of comparison created by the media. Social media especially can leave you feeling "less-than."

This was true for me, as well. When I lived in Vancouver, bulimia would come and go depending on how well I was coping with life and how my need for significance was being met. Rockin' my career? In a budding new relationship? Speaking at conferences? Climbing some high mountain? Serving on various boards? My Ed would ebb. But when I moved to Phoenix to be with my now husband, my sense of significance plummeted. I felt essentially alone in a new city (he worked 12 hour days), had very few close friends, no family, and no longer my award-winning real estate career. I was also thrust into a world of global leaders and high-level entrepreneurs. In my career in Vancouver, I had been a big-ish fish in a tiny pond. Now I felt like algae in a vast ocean. My Ed was a way out of the feelings of inadequacy, uncertainty, and loneness, and it began to rage worse than ever. Days and days were spent alone filled with multiple cycles, but a sense of significance would never come out of that. I was just burying my lack thereof.

Variety

You can get so stuck in a rut with your existing life structures, activities, and habits that you seek variety in any number of ways, including unsupportive food choices. Rather than getting more creative in how you use your time, you get creative in the foods you eat. But the creation is usually riddled with fat, salt, sugar, and preservatives. Not a pretty picture.

I can see how this need for variety also drove my bulimia in a number of ways. My daily patterns were the same—work, play, have unbearable emotions, experience the need to escape, gather my medicine, ingesting it, purge, feel peace, repeat. It became predictable day after day. And with no one to be accountable to, the cycle perpetuated.

The need for variety was also there in my food choices. So many "fattening" foods were taboo growing up, and lord knows you couldn't be fat in my family (the first nursery rhyme I recall my dad saying was "fatty, fatty, two by four, couldn't get through the kitchen door." He would also point out larger people and conversely look at me and say, "Don't worry, you can't fatten a thoroughbred.") He was not a malicious person by any means, just highly body focused.

So much pressure and subsequent food restriction might have been the catalyst for the need for variety to eventually kick in. *Eat taboo foods, damn it! But, I better not gain an ounce, so just become bulimic.* And that's what I did. How is the variety in your life? Try to create as much of it as you can, so it doesn't become a driving force for your bulimia.

Connection

You are a social animal, and connection is fundamental to your survival. You live in the most technologically connected era, yet it's perhaps the loneliest version of society ever experienced. Disconnection caused by technology aside, even if you are face-to-face and not screen-to-screen, the glass wall of your bulimia is always between you and any chance to connect. At a social gathering, it's as if you're looking into a giant, vibrant, life-affirming aquarium from your little island of dry land. You're here. They're there. The wall is invisible, but it is deeply sensed. Friends can't put their finger on why you seem disconnected, but it's undeniable. You see them as schools of fish on the other side of the glass swimming happily and connecting with one another, and you want to be with them. But you don't speak their language nor breathe water. You desperately want the barrier broken, but you have no idea how to live without it. You feel as if breaking that glass will bring a tsunami of water, sharks, fish, and piranhas. You will surely die.

So you eventually use food because certain foods have the capacity to make you feel a sense of connection. Does ice cream remind you of those carefree childhood moments, licking cones with your buddies? Now ice cream replaces the friends. Does chocolate conjure up memories of sitting across from your best girlfriend, sharing a Cadbury bar and your hearts. Chocolate later becomes a personal counselor and confidant. Does popcorn produce mental pictures of your family movie nights? Now, popcorn promises you a pretend feeling of bonding.

My bulimia started when I felt the loneliest and most disconnected. After spending time at my college boyfriend's home and experiencing the familial connection there, the lack of it I felt at home became unbearable. I pondered all the times my dad was absent before he left for good when I was ten, the years my mom had to work late so no one was home, older siblings busy with their own lives, the sometimes tense moments in our new blended family, and the decades of feeling lost. The feelings cascaded and my realization that I was essentially alone in this world became unbearable. I'm not saying I was alone. There were people around sometimes. But I felt alone and food filled the void.

The important thing to recognize is that certainty, significance, variety, and connection are emotional needs that cannot be satisfied by food, but that often drive your food choices. They sure did mine.

Recognizing Emotional Hunger

Understanding emotional hunger's roots is helpful, but other than a growl in the stomach, how you really know if hunger is emotional or physical? Do you want to eat because your body needs food or because your emotions need comforting? Emotional eating is defined as "the practice of consuming large quantities of food—usually comfort or junk foods—in response to feelings instead of hunger."

In her book *Constant Craving: What Your Food Cravings Mean and How to Overcome Them*, Doreen Virtue further explains the eight ways to determine if hunger is emotional or physical. I found this comparison helpful.

Emotional Hunger	Physical Hunger
Comes on suddenly.	Is gradual.
Is for a very specific food.	Is open to different foods.
Begins in the mouth and mind.	Starts in the stomach.
Is urgent.	Is patient.
Is paired with upsetting emotions.	Occurs out of a physical need for food.
Involves automatic or absentminded eating.	Involves conscious and aware eating.
Does not notice the physical feeling of fullness.	Stops when full.
Causes guilt.	Realizes eating is as important as breathing. There is no guilt.

I hope you can start to really get in touch with the various types of emotional hunger so you can begin to get those needs met in more effective and lasting ways. Bulimia will tell you it's the answer in the moment, but it always lies.

Three Outcomes for a Bulimic

As with drug or alcohol addiction, in my view, there are three outcomes for bulimia:

1. Die of your disease.
2. Kill yourself.
3. Quit.

The first two options may seem harsh, but you simply cannot abuse your mind and body continually without fairly drastic consequences. According to the National Association of Anorexia Nervosa and Associated Disorders (ANAD), every 62 minutes, at least one person in America dies as a direct result of an eating disorder. They also cite that eating disorders have the highest mortality rate for any mental illness (not that I or many experts believe eating disorders are necessarily a mental illness). The National Eating Disorder Association (NEDA), reports that the mortality rate for anorexia nervosa is 4% and the mortality rate for bulimia nervosa is 3.9%. This 3.9% statistic is based solely on data from death certificates in the United States listing bulimia as the cause of death—cardiac arrest and other common health issues among those suffering with bulimia are frequently cited instead of the eating disorder itself. If I had died of a heart attack for example, bulimia would not have been recorded as the cause of death since, early on, no one knew I was bulimic. Given this nuance in medical records, some research shows the mortality rate for bulimics is as high as 10%. There is also a high suicide rate in bulimia nervosa.

I finally decided—I better quit.

Looking back, I see my addictions were all interrelated. If one was dormant, another raged. If one enabled me to cope, another was unnecessary. If one had control over me, another could relax. One thing is certain though, from the time I was 15 years old and smoking a pack a day, until I was 44 and finally quit bulimia, I was an addict. The binge/purge cycle was simply the addiction that finally broke my ego and led me to my soul.

My outcome was eventually option number three and yours can be, too.

Freedom Exercises

1. In your journal, write the word **Certainty**. Then take a minute to ponder where in your life you are feeling uncertain. Write down what comes to mind. Now ponder each circumstance, and ask yourself if you have any power or control over moving the needle to a place of certainty. For example, you may be feeling uncertain about the results of a medical exam you had last week, so you can choose to pick up the phone, call your doctor, and get the results. This action you have power over. You may be uncertain about your job security, so you can reach out to your manager and request a review to be scheduled. You may be living on a month-to-month lease, but you can propose a 12-month term to your landlord. Some places of uncertainty can be rectified. Do those things. For those items you have no power over, for example, the *results* of the medical exam, whether your company will be viable long-term, or whether your landlord will renew your lease or not, try to come to a place of acceptance and gratitude for what is. Try your best to be okay in the areas of uncertainty where you have absolutely no control or power. Food will never provide you with the needed sense of certainty. You can attempt to eat uncertainty away, but it never works.

2. Next write down **Significance** and work through the same process. Where are you feeling insignificant and possibly using food to create a sense of significance? Ask yourself how you can, in a healthy way, begin to create feelings of significance. This can be as simple as going to your local SPCA to walk stray

dogs, as long-term as finishing the book you started writing, or as immediate and deep as finding a local kundalini yoga class or Transcendental Meditation school where you can really tap into Source. This will bring you a soul-level knowing that your very *being* is significant.

3. Next write down **Variety** and ask yourself, where are you stuck in a rut? List a handful of examples and commit to doing the opposite of these things for the next week—or longer. Variety is a basic human need, and if you are not getting it in your life, you can attempt to satisfy it with food. You have the power to create variety, and it could be one of the keys to quitting bulimia.

4. Now do the same for **Connection**. Write down where you are feeling disconnected. This is likely the biggest category of change as bulimia and other eating disorders are so isolative. Even if you are at a social event or dinner party and attempting to connect, your mind is often elsewhere, and your anxiety is likely inhibiting you from being truly present. Make a list of things you can do to connect with others that do not involve food—walks, volunteering, meeting for tea, book clubs, or foreign language MeetUps. Make it a point to put one new non-food related event on your calendar this week that will provide you with a sense of safe connection.

CHAPTER 3

FREEDOM STRATEGY 1: SHARING YOUR SECRET

"The only way we can live is if we grow.
The only way we can grow is if we change.
The only way we can change is if we learn.
The only way we can learn is if we are exposed.
And the only way we can become exposed
is if we throw ourselves out into the open.
Do it. Throw yourself."
—C. JoyBell C.

I was 44 years old and still had my head in the toilet most days. I had been counseling with Cesar consistently for about 3 months, but I had told my husband, Ken, it was simply to help me through the major transition over the previous few years—I had moved from Vancouver to Phoenix, had gone from being single to being married, my once lucrative award-winning career in Canada was now a more creative entrepreneurial one, and I had gone from 100% financial freedom and independence to having very little personal income. In short, I said I was lost in my new life and needed help finding my way.

I kept from Ken my *main* reason for going to counseling, as I didn't feel safe enough with that wounded and messed up part of my heart yet. It was so tender and raw, and I wasn't sure he could handle it. And if he could handle it, I wasn't sure if he would use it against me in the future. (If there were ever relationship issues, he might blame me because I was wacko.) So I kept quiet. Even though he knew I would tell Ken when I was ready, week after week, Cesar gently challenged me to do so. Eventually, it became crystal clear that in order for me to succeed in abstinence I had to share my secret with my life partner. So I did.

One night over dinner, I plucked up the courage to tell Ken I was binging and purging and couldn't stop. I shared the previous 20+ years of up and down struggles culminating in the last few that were close to the worst ever. This "part of my past he knew about" was suddenly right on our doorstep and facing us down. It was a present day reality, and sharing it felt like a heart meld. It was freeing and humiliating and bonding. Here I was, a high functioning, successful, smart, outwardly happy person who had her head in the toilet most days. I felt crazy. But I was met with love and acceptance. He even said, "Big deal! Don't give it so much power. Everybody has some coping mechanism or the other." Really? This was amazing.

He was right—I wasn't crazy. And you aren't either. In fact as an addict, you are likely often viewed as a liar, but you are actually a radical truth teller given the right timing. Not only are you a radical truth teller, your addiction is also—it tells you there is something wrong in your soul, in your life, in your family, in your circle of friends, even in the world. Your behaviors are screaming for you to examine, to challenge, to ponder. Bulimia is a truth teller, and once you consciously join the conversation about your struggles, life will get better.

Coming clean to Ken was the second time in my life I had fessed up that I was really struggling. The first time I told someone about my bulimia was via a short note. I just didn't have the courage to say it face to face. My dad was flying from Vancouver to Oregon, where he lived. As I left him at the airport in Vancouver, I handed him a Manila envelope and said, "Please don't open it until you're on the plane." As I walked away, I started to panic, knowing he would be calling me in a few short hours. I wasn't sure what he would say, but I knew fessing up was mandatory for my survival. I was 26 years old.

The envelope contained a note saying I was bulimic, I couldn't quit, and it was going to take me out if I didn't get help. I also included a brochure for Remuda Ranch over which I'd scrawled—*this is where I need to go*. It seemed it was one of the first times in my life I actually reached out for help. Once I had, the dam of secrecy and shame broke and my healing journey gushed into reality.

I'm sure my dad immediately called my mom who immediately called my best girlfriend who immediately came over and showered me with love. The release of finally sharing my secret opened the floodgates. Tears wouldn't stop. It was like a nervous breakdown. Maybe it was one. Vanessa gently washed my hair as I sat in the bathtub and wept. This kind of vulnerability-induced tenderness was previously non-existent in my life. It felt awkwardly beautiful.

My parents basically handled most of the logistics—calling the owner of the restaurants I managed saying I wouldn't be in on Monday, notifying my landlord I wouldn't be renewing the lease, booking movers to take my things to storage, packing up my apartment, and arranging travel. I was a wreck. Shame tried to cover me—I wanted to hide from the world—but I also felt freer than ever. My everything-was-okay façade crumbled, and seeing the pile of rubble was a relief. It had become way too heavy to wear.

Whom Do You Trust?

One thing I know for sure—you cannot heal in isolation. Eventually, you will simply have to pluck up the courage and trust someone enough to share your struggle with bulimia. Even if you're not sure you're ready to leave your eating disorder behind just yet, coming clean is still an important step. And sharing could be the catalyst you need to get serious. If you know exactly who to contact, make the call. But if your bulimia has isolated you to such a degree you don't even know who to contact, take a pen and paper, spend a few quiet minutes in prayer and meditation, and record the names that come to you. Your prayer can be as simple as, *Spirit/Universe/Mother Nature/God*—whomever you feel comfortable praying to—*please bring to mind the person who's already prepared to hear my story.*

Sit quietly for a minute or two and wait.

Then write down what comes to you. Don't edit and don't be surprised if certain names seem random—people you haven't even spoken with for a while. Have faith in the answers. Then ponder each person, asking the following questions:

- Can I trust this person with my heart?
- Is this a healthy person in her own life?
- Is this someone I can see walking closely with for the next six months or more?
- Do I feel good in my body and soul when I think of this person?
- Does this person tend to gossip?

Obviously you want the first four questions to be answered with a "yes" and the last with a "no." If the person tends towards gossip, no matter how many times they swear they will keep quiet, they likely won't have the capacity. During this tender time, it's imperative you feel safe. If you sense your confidant is spreading your story, the possible shame and uncertainty around who also may be in your "private" loop may lead you back to bulimia. Best to keep sharing to a minimum during this stage of recovery. Sharing shamelessly and deeply with many others will come later, but it is your story to tell— -no one else's.

If there is literally no one that comes to mind, please feel free to reach out to me at RatherthanRehab.com. I would be honored to help you on your road to recovery.

Deeper Levels of Authenticity

In my late 20s, I experienced some level of sketchy abstinence and was invited to speak at women's conferences, churches, and other smaller gatherings. Radical truth telling became my commitment as I shared my recovery story publically. I could see the difference it was making in the lives of many women. After a talk, invariably people would approach me with details of either their eating disorder struggle or their daughter's or their friend's. My honesty brought opportunities to help others, which made the years of struggle worth it. But when I fully relapsed, that all changed. I became hopeless once again.

I went to every length I knew to quit, but just couldn't. I scoured books, went to recovery meetings, prayed, served, and reached out to others for support. At one point I even went to the elders of my church and had them anoint me with oil and pray over me. Desperation drove me, and I believed the bible's promise that if I did this act of faith and humility, I would be healed. These five older men in suits and ties must have thought I was nuts. "I binge eat then throw up and can't stop doing it," I told them. "Um, okay, let's pray," they responded as they dabbed my forehead with oil from a small vial. I'm sure this was a first for them. I even went to a spiritual healer to be exorcised. Maybe I *was* possessed? Nothing worked. I had no idea about emotional hunger, nutritional hunger, addiction, or pain avoidance in those days. I was still trying to rip off the Band-Aid of bulimia in the hopes it would miraculously vanish.

After my radical failure at living free from bulimia in my 20s and 30s, I stopped reaching out for help and stopped sharing about my addiction. How could I have? Years of talking about it would have made me tired of my own voice. I only became willing to talk about it once I was actually abstinent and able to spread hope. Sharing while still stuck in the thick of dysfunction just felt embarrassing, heavy, and a waste of words.

That all changed years later when faced with my lack of authenticity. I was participating in a self-expression and leadership program, and the evening's topic was something about authenticity and the masks we wear in order to keep safe. Wham. It dawned on me during the talk that the masks we wear actually shield us from being known and therefore from being loved. If people love us only for what they see on the outside, but we have this secret flaw, we will always wonder, *would they really love me if they fully knew me?* So in a paradoxical way, hiding the flaw in order to be loved, keeps us from the very unconditional love we crave.

I decided to take the stage that night in an open share time and tell about a hundred people that I was struggling with bulimia. I said it was one of the protective masks I wore and that my commitment to living authentically basically forced me to fess up. Gulp. What would all these people think of me? I was still so wrapped up in needing people to like and accept me. To approve. But I have zero control over that, nor do you. The sooner we can let go of needing approval, the sooner we can get on with being the person we were created to be.

My concerns that night were unfounded. Many people came up to me after the event to share their story with the same or similar struggles. In a one-on-one share time later during the evening, the man I was paired up with even shared *his* story of bulimia and that my speaking out gave him the courage to also come clean. It made us both cry. Bulimia seems to be such a "woman's" disorder, but the statistics are that 10% of bulimics are men. My guess is the reality is higher as men seem to be less likely to share their story or seek help for their addiction to bulimia. Therefore many male strugglers don't even show up in the statistics.

Arm Yourself with Resources

Before I could come clean with anyone when I was 26, I needed to understand what I was facing and if there was any way I could navigate recovery privately. As mentioned before, I hit the library, scoured for books on the topic, and read about various healing modalities. I spent hours reading there because I was too embarrassed to actually check out the books. And what if my roommate found them? One book that especially impacted me back then was, *The Monster Within, Overcoming Bulimia* by Cynthia Rowland McClure. Just reading her story in that first edition of her book gave me hope. I wasn't alone. Up until that point, I had only known one other person who had bulimia, and it happened to have been one of my best girlfriends in high school. She had suddenly become quite thin, and one night we caught her purging. A few of us gently confronted her, but when nothing changed, we went to her parents so they could get her the help she needed. She eventually got well. I couldn't believe I was in my mid-20s and caught in the same cycle.

After reading every book the library offered, I broadened my search to include treatment centers. My search for something local came up empty. I guess Vancouver was not the epicenter for bulimia recovery in the mid-1990s. But I did find a treatment center in Wickenberg, AZ. Going to rehab was radical, but it seemed I really needed it.

Thankfully, today effective resources are available without disrupting your life with rehab. You can likely find an Eating Disorders Anonymous support group within six miles of your home, you can easily find a qualified on-line/telephone recovery coach, and you can certainly order recovery related books via Amazon and have them delivered to the privacy of your own home. Back then, this was not the case. Help was so much harder to find. So take courage, you are in the perfect time and place to successfully heal from your eating disorder without a massive level of disruption.

Freedom Exercises

1. Do your best to become willing to reach out to at least one safe person from your list, and share your struggle. Let them know you have no expectation of them—you simply want to bring your secret out into the open, and you love and trust them enough with it. Ask them for confidentiality for now, and tell them you will be sharing with others, as you feel safe to do so. You will be surprised as you share. More people than you can ever imagine have or are also now struggling with similar issues. This conversation can be the catalyst for a deep connection to develop. If sharing is too scary at this moment, just begin to visualize yourself sharing at some point in the near future, when you feel safe to do so. Visualizing can evaporate the fear.

2. Sit quietly and breathe deeply for three minutes, twice each day, morning and evening. Inhale for five counts, gently hold for five counts, exhale for five counts, then rest with your lungs empty for the last five counts. Repeat as many times as needed to take you to at least three minutes. Ideally you will work up

to ten minutes, but start with three. This 20 count breathing exercise will ground and calm you. Recovery can be a stressful time, so breathing exercises will help mitigate the impact on your nervous system.

CHAPTER 4

FREEDOM STRATEGY 2: HEALING OPTIONS FOR MAXIMUM SUCCESS

"Growth is a detox process, as our weakest, darkest places
are sucked up to the surface in order to be released."
—Marianne Williamson

In October of 1995 after returning home from five months in rehab, I was faced with having to design a program of long-term recovery. Gone were the walls and locks and people rationing out my food and controlling my exercise. Gone were the daily counseling sessions, equine therapy, and being with sisters who totally understood. Back home it was real-life recovery, and I was petrified.

A quote in the Big Book of Alcoholics Anonymous says, "Half measures availed us nothing." In other words, you need to play the recovery game full out. Trying to overcome your eating disorder half-heartedly will not work. But don't be afraid. You will be victorious. Your pain will not be wasted. Go all-in and you'll get there. Remember, you've simply been trying to get legitimate needs met in an illegitimate way, and once you learn how to get your needs met without using food, you'll be free from the obsession.

Be gentle on yourself.

At the same time, you have to commit 100% to the game, no shortcuts, no fooling yourself or anyone else. In this chapter, I'll share specific tools for various stages of recovery that will help you build solid abstinence. Some will seem contradictory, and some will fit like puzzle pieces. All are valuable. I encourage you to read each section, and see which resonates most. You can use each in a linear fashion as I did, or you may bounce around from one to another as your soul indicates. Either way is okay. As long as the end result is full and final recovery, you are on the right road.

Treatment Centers

People I work with who are new in recovery often ask, "Are treatment centers helpful? Necessary? Frivolous?" These are very good questions, and the answers can go either way depending on the circumstances. In her book *Inside Rehab: The Surprising Truth About Addiction Treatment—and How to Get Help That Works*, Anne Fletcher demonstrates how ineffective short-term treatment can be without proper aftercare and how those with long-term abstinence are recovering successfully in their natural environment, through the support of trusted relationships, empowering surroundings, and healthy behaviors. In other words, rather than going to rehab, they are building life-long recovery at home.

I fully agree, as you may have guessed by the title of this book. My five-month stay at Remuda Ranch didn't usher in my recovery, it was everything I did post-treatment that eventually did. Plus, it was wildly expensive. Treatment centers run in the $1,500-3,000 per day range, so the cost is enough to choke you. But if you aren't able to live one day to the next without binging and purging, you are afraid you may harm yourself, or the situation at home is unbearable, a treatment center can be helpful. It can be the line in the sand, so to speak, between your old life and your new life. But just know—rehab is not a magic event that will snap you into recovery. Real recovery starts when you get out.

My time at Remuda Ranch was a small part of my healing, but in the moment, it seemed mandatory. I was scared for my wellbeing. I was alone. I was living a secret. I was ashamed. And in that pre-Internet era, I didn't know where else to turn. Thanks to treatment, I went from not being able to eat even one item without it turning into a binge/purge episode to actually holding down all but one meal for five months. But this really wasn't the victory it seems—I was in lock-down and watched 24/7. The nurses flushed our toilets for one hour after each meal. Yup, we had personal toilet flushers. Some of the girls giggled at the lovely packages they would save up all morning to deliver to the nurses after their lunch. The things you do to entertain yourself.

One thing you *might* love about rehab is the complete lack of stress around food and weight. All control is removed so you have no responsibility for your intake or your weight gain. I understood enjoying the lack of control over food, but my reaction to weight gain surprised me. While I hated it, I justified it as being their fault. They told me when, what, and how much to eat, so I had zero power. Heaven. Would you like that? Or would that be scary? Many girls loved it. Many didn't. The daily weigh-ins were stressful—the resulting number would dictate our food plan for the next few days. Some girls would put rocks in their underwear hoping their meals would be altered accordingly.

One question I wanted answered before even being admitted was, "How much weight will you make me gain?" Of course, they would never say. There was no magic number. It all depended on the severity of each person's eating disorder. Statistically, most bulimics are at or even above a healthy weight, so many girls found they even shed pounds in treatment. But they categorized me as bulimarexic, meaning I was bulimic *and* below a healthy weight, so I knew I'd be on a gaining program. Whether you go to rehab or not, don't worry about weight gain. Trust in the process. The more you focus on weight, the less you are available for healing. Your body will normalize once it begins to trust you with its wellbeing.

Another positive aspect of a treatment center is that it's really hard to harm yourself. If you feel like you might do something drastic, rehab could be a good option. Upon arrival, you are basically strip-searched. Nothing gets through that could be deemed harmful to you or your recovery—no belts, razors, or even baby oil, which I learned some people use as a laxative. If you're a smoker, this will be a great chance to cut down or quit as your cigarettes are rationed.

They remove many of your external coping mechanisms so you can do the deep inner work of recovery. One-on-one therapy, group therapy, art therapy, equine therapy, body image therapy—it was all mandatory. And helpful. Maybe for the first time, you will be with other souls who know exactly the pain you are in and also trying desperately to avoid. Your stories will all be different, but according to the experts, three common threads form the braid of your bulimia—self-starvation, anxiety, and a lack of familial connection.

The first two seem obvious, but the third was an idea I had avoided analyzing or accepting. I didn't want to look at my disappointments. I didn't want to look back. I didn't want to feel. How are your familial relationships? Do you sense you are valued? Understood? Are you heart connected with those in your family of origin or with your current nuclear family? Do you feel safe? Secure? I ask because psychologists have called eating disorders family diseases. Were you a particularly sensitive child? Did you pick up on the household dynamics even before you were old enough to understand them? Did you internalize any dysfunction and try to cope using some means or another? Not to place blame on anyone or anything—a lack of familial connection is just something counselors and experts see repeatedly.

I'm personally convinced that someone's home life could have been perfect, and she still might have manifested an eating disorder. Disconnection from her peers at school, from her colleagues at work, or from her own soul might have had her seek out destructive pain avoidance strategies. Either way, the resulting discomfort could simply be the necessary pathway to her soul's enlightenment. Spirit doesn't waste a thing.

Eating disorders can be used for deep healing for both the sufferer and the entire family as they often blow up the image of the "perfect" home life where everything is okay, everyone is happy, and everyone is connected. There is no blame here. Everything is just the way it's supposed to be. I believe you choose exactly the parents and the family situation you needed to learn the lessons your soul came to Earth to learn. So gratitude is really the only response. You are perfectly where you are supposed to be and so is each member of your family. When I look at familial turmoil and disconnection, I always think of a book. Today is only one chapter. It's not the conclusion. Be grateful. Be forgiving. Be the example.

I left Remuda knowing I was not alone, I was not a freak, and that there were very good reasons for my harmful coping mechanisms. That was helpful. But when I returned home to Vancouver, I was physically alone and relapsed badly. In treatment, they identified I was also an alcoholic—I failed the AA test miserably or passed with flying colors, whichever way you want to look at it. So when I got home, not only was I trying to stop using food to ease my pain and anxiety, I couldn't drink either. And no drinking meant no hanging around with my group of friends. Drinking was just part of our lives. My dad, stepmom, and sister all lived in a different country. My mom and stepdad had left for their annual six-month winter holiday shortly after I returned home. And my brother was busy with his own life, so I found myself feeling increasingly alone and anxious. Bulimia became my only solace, and it raged worse than it ever had before rehab.

The time I spent there, while helpful in the moment, sure didn't equip me to make the courageous choices staring down food, anxiety, and loneliness on my own. One recovery non-negotiable is becoming skilled at sitting with uncomfortable emotions. Just being with them. Feeling them. Processing them. Looking back, we were kept so busy in rehab that we never really learned to deal with real and raw emotions in the moment of choice.

Viktor E. Frankl, holocaust survivor and author, says, "Between stimulus and response there is a space. In that space is our power to choose our response. In our response lies our growth and our freedom." This is the piece that was missing in the treatment center. There were no choices. They were all made for us. What we did, when we ate, how we exercised, and what we flushed. The opportunity to grow and truly live in freedom was thwarted by rules and restrictions, and because we weren't being bulimic or we had gained a little weight, we seemed better than we actually were.

Treatment Center Pros:
- Protection from yourself
- Time and support to do the deep work of recovery
- Surrounded by peers who understand you and your struggles

Treatment Center Cons:
- So protected that you aren't really flexing the recovery muscle—making the choice to abstain when faced with the freedom to binge/purge
- Very expensive

- Disrupts your life in a major way
- Temporary support

AA, OA and EDA

While a treatment center can provide you with a temporary solution to your bulimia, real recovery happens at home. It happens in the moments you're socializing with friends and choose to be present and eat healthily. It happens when you are driving home and choose to either pass by your favorite binge food store without stopping or take an alternate route. And it often happens in a community of like-minded sojourners, which is where Alcoholics Anonymous (AA), Overeaters Anonymous (OA) and Eating Disorders Anonymous (EDA) come into the picture.

When I returned from Remuda Ranch in 1995, EDA had not even been founded yet, so my only choices to work through the 12-steps were within AA and OA. And while I was a very active member in AA for 41/2 years, I never really felt I could process my food issues there. In OA groups, I was usually the only normal-weighted woman, and there were enough little side comments that I didn't feel understood or part of the fellowship. I just wanted to scream, "I'm just like you! The only difference is I can't stand an ounce of extra flesh on my body so I throw up my binges! And I hate my body as much as you say you hate yours." I did say as much, but I was still brushed aside as if I had nothing to work through since I was thin, accepted by society, and didn't need a seatbelt extender.

Thankfully, EDA was created in 2000 and subsequently flourished. I found hope in those rooms with my sisters in recovery. I highly recommend you find a group in your area, and connect with women suffering with the same behaviors as you. Make sure the group you commit to has a number of women with long-term abstinence and that the general feeling of the group is positive, hopeful, and uplifting.

There are some groups who simply aren't quite ready and spend the hour commiserating about their slips and their despair.

Working through the 12-steps, on the other hand, will be no different from one group to the next—it's your work. I'm incredibly grateful for EDA as it was a huge part of my recovery. While I never did achieve long-term abstinence through AA back in 1995 and beyond, working a 12-step program helped me begin to like myself again. And that was a start. But EDA in 2012 was the beginning of genuine and solid recovery. A link to its website is in the resource section at the end of this book. I suggest you find a group in your area—you will meet friends there that may last a lifetime. You may even meet your own soul there if you're open. One thing I know for sure, recovery on your own will be next to impossible. Recovery with people around you, spurring you on and supporting you, is a given.

While there are many wildly positive aspects of 12-step programs during certain parts of recovery, a pivotal part of mine was leaving the formal "anonymous" meetings behind once I sensed they were no longer serving my recovery. Once in 2000 and once in 2013.

After doing the 12-step work diligently in AA for 41/2 years—I felt it was starting to hold me back. I had my eye on true freedom, and the fear I was under in AA wasn't consistent with that target. So I did an experiment in a very controlled environment. I planned on having my first glass of wine in 41/2 years among trusted friends at a special event the following weekend. My then sponsor, Lois, freaked out. "Don't do it! You'll lose your five year cake!" In AA, the milestones are celebrated and important, but my freedom was even more so.

That Saturday night, I chose to have a drink. I ordered a white wine spritzer, which took me longer to drink than a double scotch would have five years prior. Then I ordered another. Halfway through that second glass, I started to feel the effects and switched to straight Perrier. I had spent a number of years working the 12-steps and actually learning to like my sober self, so I didn't need an alcohol-induced personality anymore.

In that stage of recovery, AA worked well for a season. Although I still disagree with a few of the steps, AA was a major log in the raft that saved my life. Never before had I met a more honest and brave group of souls, and they helped me get honest and brave, too. In 2012, the members of EDA did also. When I got serious about recovering from bulimia in my early 40s, EDA was a lifeline. Walking into my first meeting and sitting around a table with about a dozen other women, all in various stages of recovery, I instantly felt at home. It uses basically the same 12 steps and 12 traditions as AA, but focuses on issues around food and body image, not alcohol. EDA is an amazing resource. There are groups all over the world as well as on-line and by telephone just waiting for you to connect. You will find acceptance, knowledge, wisdom, tools, accountability, and love. I'm so thankful for my 20th Street and Campbell Monday night EDA group, and I send any new person I'm working with to these meetings. The rooms, the brave souls, and the connections—they are invaluable. Maybe for a season, maybe forever. Only you will know what works best for you.

12-Step Program Pros:
- Accountability and camaraderie
- Set structure for doing the deep work of recovery
- On-going and supportive program
- Abundance of meeting possibilities
- Anonymity
- Affordable as meeting attendance is by donation

12-Step Program Cons:
- Members usually identify with their disease for a lifetime
- Members can become meeting junkies, unable to cope in the "real world"

- Members' passions can get put on the back burner as their lives become so recovery focused
- Can breed fear rather than full freedom

Rational Recovery

I loved my EDA group, even though a few things about the program didn't align with my beliefs. The notion of powerlessness, having to attend meetings for a lifetime, and the theory of once-an-addict-always-an-addict never resonated. While I went to meetings, worked the steps, served, had sponsors, and mentored newcomers, I was always researching other methodologies to augment my abstinence. I believed 100% freedom was available and attending recovery meetings and doing the steps continually and forever didn't seem like freedom to me. That's when I stumbled upon Rational Recovery (RR), Jack Trimpey's profound theories on curing substance addiction. It rang as the crystal-clear truth.

The main tenant of RR is that *you* are responsible. You are *not* powerless. In fact, you hold *all* the power as you are a person filled with spirit, chutzpah, resolve, and, well, power. RR teaches, "Look at your hands, which are necessary to consume alcohol, [food], or drugs. Understand they are under your complete control at all times." Continually labeling yourself as a powerless bulimic seems to me to be keeping you in perpetual negative energy.

RR also deems recovery is an *event*, not a *process* as with EDA. My personal opinion is that in the case of alcohol or drug addiction, yes, recovery can be an event. Just never drink again from this day forward. Never smoke another joint. Never pop another pill. But in the case of food addiction, you still have to eat numerous times every day for the rest of your life. Given this reality, I think it's a lot harder to pinpoint eating disorder recovery as an event. You could go crazy asking yourself questions like, "Did I overeat at lunch?" "Am I out of recovery?" "Was that extra cookie considered a binge?" To avoid this kind of subjective and potentially obsessive questioning, your *event* can simply be as mine was: the day you stopped purging.

As I secured some solid recovery, my feelings towards the structure of EDA began to change. The freedom it provided in the beginning had flipped to feeling like my wings were being clipped. I no longer wanted to identify with powerlessness, but rather with the power espoused in the teachings of RR. Adopting these new recovery theories felt as if had I been swept off a long, confusing, and convoluted dirt road and placed on a clear, straight, and uncomplicated conveyer belt. As I walked purposefully, I was also being carried effortlessly towards recovery. Totally opposite from what EDA literature suggests, RR teaches, "Don't hang around with recovery groupers. Form new relationships based on common interests (passions!) rather than common problems." This made sense, and I eventually moved on from those meetings. I still maintain some wonderful EDA friendships, but have adopted Rational Recovery as my core belief system for achieving addiction abstinence. Using its tools brought me ever closer to full freedom from bulimia, and I hope you'll explore it also.

Rational Recovery Pros:
- Breeds freedom over fear
- No time consuming meetings
- Encourages you to take full responsibility for your recovery
- You are not identified or labeled as your past behaviors

Rational Recovery Cons:
- No accountability and camaraderie
- No on-going support or structure
- No meetings

Professional Counseling

One-on-one professional counseling, whether for an extended or brief time period, can be invaluable in helping you break the binge/ purge habit. The structure of set appointments, specific assignments, and weekly weaning challenges help bring recovery into the absolute forefront of your life—things get real with this level of accountability and support.

There is no science to finding the right person—you can simply Google counselors in your area and peruse the on-line reviews, you can ask someone in your EDA recovery group for references, or you can call a respected treatment center for a referral. If you choose in-person sessions, it will be wise to find someone convenient—the fewer obstacles, the more likely you will be to use her regularly. Of course you have to feel comfortable with your therapist, so asking for a short personal meeting before jumping into a package of paid sessions is perfectly acceptable. Your soul will need to feel safe, so choose wisely. Then trust your choice and commit.

While Cesar always armed me with exercises, things to ponder, and assignments to complete, the main benefit to hiring him was accountability. I had extensive head knowledge and had done years of healing work already, so I simply needed to start getting real about slowing down and eventually stopping the bulimic behaviors. That was my commitment and, under Cesar's care, the periods of freedom got increasingly long until freedom simply became my life. One day, I wrote in my journal:

I had a 12-day stretch with no BP!!

That was a miracle. Later I wrote:

It's been 4+ months since I've BP'ed. So proud of myself!!

I really was proud of myself as abstinence was previously impossible. Can you imagine going that long without using your bulimia to cope? I know you will be able to once you commit wholeheartedly to freedom and then get proficient in using the recovery tools available.

Professional Counseling Pros:
- Personalized recovery program
- Accountability
- Professional accreditation

Professional Counseling Cons:
- Expensive
- Therapist may have no personal experience with bulimia
- Can spend so much time digging up the past that you forget to focus on creating an amazing future

Certified Addiction Recovery Coaching

While a professional counselor can be invaluable for your healing, so can a Certified Addiction Recovery Coach. This is a person highly experienced and trained in addiction recovery, but who does not hold a Masters Degree in such. I wasn't aware of this specialty in early recovery and would have certainly used one had I been.

There are many differences between a professional therapist and a recovery coach. Firstly, a Certified Addiction Recovery Coach has usually walked the recovery road herself, knows the path intimately, and loves helping others as they find their own way to freedom. Also, while recovery coaching is a highly professional relationship, the exchange of conversation seems more peer-to-peer than professional-to-patient, which feels very uplifting and hopeful. Another difference between addiction recovery coaching and counseling is the focus—with coaching, it is on achieving abstinence and living the best life possible, not necessarily on digging up the past to better understand the present. The goal in recovery coaching is also holistic health, not just addition abstinence, even though they usually go hand in hand.

A few years into my own eating disorder abstinence, I hired a certified addiction recovery coach to fine-tune my freedom with food and my body image issues. It was invaluable. Eric's beautiful blend of empathy and tough love provided me with the safety, accountability, and compassion I needed. He inspired me to get certified to coach others in the same professional capacity as well.

Certified Addiction Recovery Coaching Pros:
- Personalized recovery program
- Accountability
- Relatable peer-to-peer relationship
- Coach usually has personal experience within the area she is coaching
- Normally over the phone, so very convenient

Certified Addiction Recovery Coaching Cons:
- Can be expensive
- Usually has no group dynamics

Plant Medicines

I'm going to touch on a very controversial topic, but one that is finally gaining popularity and acceptance in North America: plant medicines. What are those, you may ask? The short answer is a deeply profound part of my, and countless others', journey to freedom. The long answer could fill volumes of books on its own, but let me give just a brief synopsis of the few I'm familiar with.

Iboga, a plant root originally discovered in Gabon, West Africa, has been used successfully for decades in the healing of hard-core addictions. Five-year post-treatment success rates have been in the 80% range for heroin and other such drug addictions. No other substance—manmade or natural—has had such a positive result. Iboga (also Ibogaine, one of the 13 alkaloids found in the Iboga root) has a rewiring effect on the brain's neuropathways. It virtually eradicates a heroin user's physical withdrawal symptoms and subsequent cravings.

While drugs were not my issue, I became interested in Iboga for its proven usefulness in freeing people from addictions, negative thought patterns, and other destructive behaviors. It can also be effective in helping people reach inner peace, heal destructive family patterns, and develop a higher level of consciousness. My experience was deeply profound, life altering, and healing. While the rituals and ceremonies in West Africa are generally more shamanic and spiritual, administration of these medicines in the west are usually performed under the highest level of medical supervision. Iboga has been listed as a controlled substance and is thus illegal in the U.S., but there are a number of wonderful facilities in Canada, Mexico, Central/South America, and globally that provide these services. Crossroads Treatment Center in Mexico is one such world-class facility.

While Iboga is prescribed widely for those struggling with addictions, ayahuasca, a healing Amazonian plant medicine, is considered ideal for those dealing with trauma (and who isn't in some way?) And the two often go hand in hand. Trauma/addiction = chicken/egg. Ayahuasca is capable of inducing altered states of consciousness ranging from mildly stimulating to extremely visionary. The after effect is a heightened awareness of your spirituality and a deepening of your connection with your true self. In the New Yorker, Ariel Levy writes, "If cocaine expressed and amplified the speedy, greedy ethos of the nineteen-eighties, ayahuasca reflects our present moment—what we might call the Age of Kale. It is a time characterized by wellness cravings, when many Americans are eager for things like mindfulness, detoxification, and organic produce, and we are willing to suffer for our soulfulness." And suffering you will. Plant medicines are not party drugs. They are serious healing agents and should be treated as such. But if taken correctly, in the right circumstances, and with a healthy mindset, they can be profoundly healing. My ayahuasca journeys were definitely such.

The last plant medicine I'll touch on is 5-MeO-DMT. Also known as The Power or The Spirit Molecule, it is an entheogen that has been used by both Central and South American shamans for thousands of years. An entheogen (derived from the Greek word meaning "generating the divine within") is any psychoactive substance that induces a spiritual experience and is aimed at spiritual development. I can say without a doubt, my 5-MeO-DMT session was my number one most profound and life-changing experience. I was left with a deep sense that I am pure love, I am one with all souls, I am safe, and I have an endless source of divinely guided wisdom. All these things fly in the face of the messages that my eating disordered brain had been trying to tell me for decades. For an essay on the details of my plant medicine experiences, please write "Plant Medicines" in the subject line at www.ratherthanrehab.com/contact.

Plant Medicine Pros:
- Provides reliable access to different states of consciousness that facilitate long-term healing
- Instantly rewires neuropathways
- Provides an awareness of love and connection that refutes the notions of un-lovability and isolation so common among those suffering with eating disorders

Plant Medicine Cons:
- Participants need to summon an extraordinary amount of courage to partake

- Since plant medicines are illegal in the U.S., traveling for the experience is mandatory
- While there have been no documented cases of long-term negative effects if taken as directed, ingesting any mind-altering medicine has its risks

Dear reader, this chapter contained a lot of information, and I sincerely hope it has helped, not hindered, your recovery. I simply want you to have the various healing options at your fingertips. Some may seem contradictory, which is not meant to be confusing. It's just that your recovery is not a static or linear undertaking. Nor are you. Please pick and choose which modalities might work for you. Don't be afraid to try one for a while, and then move to another. This is your life. Use your intuition to guide you. Over the decades I have had hundreds of conversations with those struggling with bulimia. No two have recovered exactly the same way, and no one has recovered alone. If you use one or more of these suggestions, if you are committed, if you have someone to be accountable to, and if you give yourself time, you will find recovery.

FREEDOM EXERCISES

1. Find an EDA group in your neighborhood, and commit to attending at least one meeting this week.
2. If you feel ready and if you connect with someone at the meeting, ask for her phone number. Then be willing to reach out as needed. Better yet, reach out before you even need to. Simply begin developing relationships with supportive people.
3. Do one thing your bulimia has caused you to put on the back burner. Whether it's calling a friend, taking your niece out for a

walk, or writing that thank you note to a friend who was there in some special way. Empower yourself to do one thing this week that you've been putting off. You will feel so much better having done it.

CHAPTER 5

FREEDOM STRATEGY 3: CLEANING HOUSE

*"The world as we have created it is a product of our thinking.
It cannot be changed without changing our thinking"*
—Albert Einstein

Albert Einstein, Wayne Dyer, Deepak Chopra, Marianne Williamson, and any other spiritual thought leader will tell you, "Change your thoughts, change your life." Well, duh! So why is it so hard? Because the monkey mind speaks loudly, quickly, and convincingly. My thoughts were definitely the pre-curser to my eating disorder. They thundered every waking moment, and they weren't pleasant. Constant self-doubt, self-criticism, self-loathing. I couldn't take the constant barrage, but I didn't know how to make it stop without using a substance. I did try to meditate, pray, read various scriptures, poems, and uplifting literature, but peace never persisted. My mind would always revert to, *You're a screw up and always will be. Look at what you do!* But every extra day I've put between my bulimia and the present has hushed that voice just a little bit more. I have a long way to go before my thoughts are 100% self-loving, but I'm heading in the right direction. I want that for you, too and I promise it's possible.

In this chapter, let's visit some practical ways you can set yourself up for success. They ultimately all start with your thinking, but you will need to alter some of your daily routines, much of your surroundings, and many of your activities as well. You may resist some of these strategies because doing them means recovery is getting real. But please follow these recommendations closely—otherwise your chance for recovery will be slim, and relapsing will be certain.

Challenge Your Thoughts

Are you ready to actively sit with and be present to your thoughts— even the painful ones—so you can truly hear them, challenge them, and ultimately change the negative ones? When an onslaught comes, try to immediately counter it with the truth. I had a constant barrage of negativity, fear, hopelessness, and self-loathing. *You're getting chunky! You'll NEVER be over bulimia. You won't amount to anything. You don't even know how to be with people, so just stay at home with your food!* When your habitual negative thoughts arise, try transforming them into positive, self-affirming ones. If your thoughts are, *You are such a failure. You'll never make the impact you want to make. You have no reason to go on. You are broken.* Change them to something like, *Your future is bright. You are here for a purpose. You are one with the Universe. You are whole, perfect, and complete.* Though a seemingly simple exercise, this will feel like some majorly heavy lifting until your personal affirmation muscles gain strength. Keep at it though. Write down your new and positive thoughts and post them any and everywhere you will see them regularly. This is not a new strategy, but actually taking the time to do it might be for you. I promise it will be worth your effort.

Detox Your Kitchen

If you're anything like I was, your pantry and fridge are bare. My kitchen was like a war zone, and nothing survived. If I planned on having friends over, I would have to shop for groceries. The half-empty mayonnaise, mustard, cocktail onions, and ketchup bottles clanging around in the door of the fridge weren't enough to offer guests. So detoxing my kitchen was easy. It was already empty. But your home may be different. There might be items lurking around calling to you, *You need me to feel better! Come eat.* But you know they are not foods that serve you. Ditch them. Give them to a food bank. Make a platter and bring them to your workplace. Whatever you do, get those temptations out of the house. Especially during early recovery.

If you live with others and some of their food triggers you, kindly ask them to bring the suspect items to their office, hide them, or keep them in their car. Seriously. Half measures availed us nothing, remember? My husband and I are at a point where we totally laugh about this. I *still* can't have certain foods around. Not that I will ever purge again, but one Pralus Le 100% chocolate square can still lead to the whole bar. There's no sugar in it anyhow, so it's okay, right? (Um, that would be Ed Light talking.) And Ken's dad's sugar-free, wheat-free, nut cookies? Forget about it. Ken literally keeps them in his trunk. Honestly. I just know those things are binge foods, and even after almost four years of abstinence I still don't trust myself with them. Ken made a batch of health cookies a few weeks ago, and every time he went to get one, he said I should leave the room. I would and we would laugh. I'd come back to him munching away and me feeling free from the powerful cookie pull. Sure, I could scour the house looking for his hiding spots—

he has many—but somehow just them being out-of-sight helps them be out-of-mind. Studies show that we will eventually give in to temptations given enough exposure to the object of desire, so do yourself a favor and detox your kitchen. Willpower is a finite resource.

Change Your Habits

Changing your habits can be a little harder as these are perhaps decade-long engraved behaviors. But in order to recover, you'll need to be diligent here. Toxic habits can be as insidious as simply the route you take home from work each day. Does it require you to drive past your favorite binge food outlet? If so, take another route. Does your habit of spending Sunday mornings snuggled in alone send you into a binge/purge episode by midday? Then make sure you plan a hike with a friend in the late morning to get you through that hump. Share with her what's going on and that her presence is a lifesaver. She will be honored. A habit might also be skipping lunch, which then sends your dinnertime hunger into grizzly bear status. Better to create a new habit of having a small and healthy bite in the middle of the day. If this is hard for you, as it was for me—lunches for some reason were a major trigger—you will likely need to develop a meditative practice around it. Another habit can be as seemingly benign as flipping through a fashion magazine while waiting in line at the grocery store or airport. But ask yourself, "How does that affect my body image? Is it helpful?" Change this habit by picking up a home décor or business magazine instead. Better yet, connect with the people around you.

There are no quick fixes to changing life-long habits, but when you start to really correlate these seemingly harmless actions, or lack thereof, as being life threatening, they will be easier to alter. If a small lunch will help you overcome a binge in the evening, won't it be worth it? If a new route home will help your abstinence, will you take it? If avoiding fashion magazines will help with your body image issues, will you refrain? Now is the time to really assess your habits. Keep the ones that work, ditch those that don't, and create new ones that support your recovery.

New Playground, New Playmates

When I got back from rehab, it became crystal clear that where I spent time, and with whom, had to radically change in order to stay abstinent. Is this true for you, too? You have thousands of conscious and subconscious associations with people and places that may ensnare you if you walk into their traps. Maybe it's the café where you meet your girlfriend every Saturday morning that smells like your mom's homemade banana bread and serves your favorite chocolate sour-cherry scones. Maybe it's the restaurant with the famous Buffalo wings, to-die-for spicy yoghourt dip, and happy hour margaritas. Maybe it's even the organic juice bar you frequent, but the full feeling from a large green smoothie always sets you up for a binge. You will know your triggers. One of mine was going to the movies. I just loved the popcorn. I would even go to the movies alone, just for the popcorn—always a large. If I didn't refill the bucket halfway through the movie, I would fill it on my way out, "For the kids, you know."

The other thing you will likely want to change is who you hang out with most of the time. What and who you surrounded yourself with got you to where you are today. So if you're ready to change, those things will likely have to change, too. Do you have friends who only want to meet at restaurants, cafes, or bars? Who can't open up about their feelings and be vulnerable? Who don't really feel safe to you, but you spend time with anyway? There may even be amazing people rocking out their lives, but are constantly amplifying your feelings of being less-than. Anyone who either pulls your body into unhealthy activities or your mind into unhealthy thoughts will have to go, even if just for a short time. Bless them for who they were to you, and either let them know or not (you will know the right thing to do in each case) that you can't spend time with them in this early stage of recovery. It can feel like rejection, so be gentle. Never judge. Each person is on her own journey and deep healing may be just around the corner for some of these people. You may even be leading the way for them. Be kind and release, with love and respect, any people who trigger you. Maybe forever, but definitely for this season of recovery.

I had to make wholesale changes. In the 1990s, most of my friends were partiers or somewhat wrapped up in body image. Many of my girlfriends had their own level of eating disorders or body dysmorphia. So early on, I chose to make new friends who seemed to be living more in line with how I wanted to live. During my final kick at the recovery can, I had less of a wholesale change to make, as my life as a married 44-year old was a lot less black and white than my life as a 26-year old. So when I finally quit bulimia in 2013, there weren't many people I really had to avoid. But I did have to *add* supportive and fun people, places, and activities. The following study will show you how vital this will be for your recovery.

Rat Park

In the 1970s, Bruce Alexander, a professor of psychology in Vancouver, B.C., published a groundbreaking study on the nature of addiction, which I find incredibly interesting and applicable to bulimia recovery. He studied caged rats provided with two water bottles—one containing pure water, the other, water laced with heroine or cocaine. The rats almost always drank the laced water and in ever increasing degrees. Close to 100% of the time, they ended up killing themselves by overdosing. That seemed to conclude the study—drug users become addicted to a substance, require increasing amounts of it, and eventually overdose. Case closed.

But is it?

Professor Alexander took the study one step further and created Rat Park. In this experiment, the rats had access to other stimuli— cheese, colored balls, tunnels, running wheels, and crucially, lots of companions. The newly formed community of rats also had access to the same two water bottles. As you may have guessed, in Rat Park, the rats almost exclusively drank only from the pure water bottle. The experiment went from the rats overdosing in almost 100% of cases to never overdosing. The differences? Community, bonding, fun, play, variety, and atmospheric beauty.

You may say, "Yes, but these are rats, not humans."

Interestingly a similar, yet accidental human experiment occurred: the Vietnam War. While abroad, an estimated 20% of troops were habitually using heroine. The fear was that when they returned to the states, there would be an epidemic of heroine addiction. Country leaders were bracing themselves for the fall out. The government anticipated needing many new programs to deal with this pending problem. But it never happened. While a small portion came home and continued drugging, most veterans returned home and resumed their lives, never to use heroine again.

If the old theory was true—that addiction was purely a physiological phenomenon—those vets should have come home hooked on drugs and should have kept using. But the medical archives show that most didn't go to rehab, didn't have physical withdrawal symptoms, and didn't keep using. They just stopped. Once they re-integrated into their lives in America, their heroine habit just stopped.

This peaked Professor Alexander's curiosity.

What if addiction isn't about the chemical hooks? What if it's about the cage? Further, what if it's about the ability to bond? Some theorize that bulimia is literally the inability to bond with others due to trauma, isolation, unmet childhood needs, and acute adult anxiety. If this is the case, our innate need to bond will drive us to bond and connect with *something* that will relieve us from our pain. This is our very nature as humans. Bonding with food is simply trying to meet a legitimate need.

Work you love, people you love, exciting things to look forward to, healthy relationships, beautiful surroundings, interesting hobbies—these are the things you might consider adding to your Rat Park. Can you do something today that will move you in the right direction? Is there something delightfully nurturing you would like to bring into your environment or a healthy habit you've been putting off cultivating? Can you do just one thing to create a life more conducive to recovery?

MeetUp for Fun

If you do need to make massive changes in your playground or playmates, I highly recommend MeetUp.com. It's a free, global on-line forum of people looking to connect with others around a common interest. And the options vary widely! If you like to basket weave with only hemp jute, I bet there's a MeetUp for you. If you like to dress up your Pug in costumes and play at a park with other Pugs, there will be a MeetUp for you. I joke, but interests can be *that* specific on MeetUp.com. Imagine a group of like-minded people getting together and gushing over their passion? It's like that sometimes. Other times, it's more conventional— hiking, biking, travel, or books clubs. Regardless of your interests, choose activities that will support your recovery. Mine were things like hiking groups, conversational French MeetUps, spirituality groups, writing guilds, and entrepreneurial clubs.

Would you be comfortable joining one of these groups and starting to meet people who have similar passions? This can be the springboard to your new life. It may seem odd at first, finding friends on-line essentially, but it's a wonderful forum. I have met a few of my closest friends through MeetUp.com.

Cross-Addiction

Besides bulimia, do you have any other behaviors or substances you just can't kick? You could be cross-addicted—most bulimics are. And those addictions could be the gateway to your bulimia. Heal one and the others follow.

I remember speaking to a spiritual counselor when I was fresh out of the treatment center, but had fallen quickly back into my old ways. He asked me, "Is there anything else you are being nudged to remove from your life? Because that very thing could be the gateway to the evil forces infiltrating and keeping you stuck." Hmmmm, I'm not so sure about evil forces *infiltrating* me, but at the time, I immediately said, "Yes, smoking." I thought to myself, *if cigarettes are keeping me in bondage to bulimia, I'll throw them away instantly.* Now, this was coming from someone who had smoked a pack-a-day since 15 years old and had never even tried to quit. Why would I have? I loved smoking. But on that day, I left his office, took my last half a pack of du Maurier reds, and dumped them in the toilet. Addiction over.

If you're anything like me, bulimia was not your first drug of choice. We did many other things to avoid pain or anxiety. But when it came time to really getting well, bulimia was near impossible to shake. I had stopped smoking, drinking, revolving-door-relationships, hell, I had even stopped sex for eight years! Yes, in my late 20s to my mid 30s, I was celibate. I was so desperate to clean up my life, and the church's teaching I was under at the time was quite adamant about pre-marital sex being "not of God." Well, okay then. I can stop if that's keeping me stuck in my eating disorder. I had already quit many other vices, so I guess sex was just another item on my road to squeaky cleanness. At the time, I thought absolute purity, as some define purity, was the path to freedom. But it was really just another form of bondage.

Today, I'm not convinced recovery is that formulaic, but I do believe cleaning up your other addictions will be highly beneficial when it comes time to cleaning up the hardest one. Someone asked me lately, which of your vices was the hardest to quit. Hands down and without skipping a beat, I said, "Bulimia." Think about it—with the other substances or activities, you can just stop and never do them again. Sure, there will be a period of white knuckling, but you won't have to win at them every moment of every day. For example, you can live without alcohol, pot, drugs, sex, relationships, shopping, the Internet— whatever your addiction—but you can't live without food. You have to face it down (at least that's how it felt early on—like some sort of O.K. Corral standoff) three or more times a day. You are surrounded by it. Food lobbyists make sure you are inundated with advertising tempting you with mouth-watering choices. It's no wonder you became bulimic. Food advertising, coupled with media's incessant portrayal of the perfect model's body —it's a wonder more people aren't where you and I ended up. Cut yourself a *lot* of slack. Then ask yourself if you have any other addictions you might consider releasing.

Your Beliefs Around Recovery

We can have all the wonderful cognitive thoughts in the world, but if our underlying belief system is faulty, we will never recover. I'll give you a non-eating disordered related example. Let's say you have a goal to earn a million dollars this year in real estate commissions. You write it down on your goals list, you put symbols of this goal on your vision board, you work backwards to see how many calls, appointments, and ultimately sales this will take, you schedule for these actions, you advertise, you empower your assistant—you do all the right things to realize this goal. But if you have negative beliefs around that goal, it will never happen. If you think, *Money is the root of all evil*, then you'll sabotage your efforts. (I realize the quote is actually "…the love of money is the root of all evil…." but I'm misquoting on purpose, as so many people do.) Another example of a competing or faulty philosophy is if you weigh, let's say

200lbs and your goal is to release 50lbs, but you tell yourself, *I come from a long line of obese people, so I will just always be obese*, can you see how you will keep yourself there? If you fundamentally disagree with your goal—and this is often entirely subconscious—your very soul will not allow you to achieve it because your soul will be going against itself.

What is your underlying belief system around your own personal recovery? Is it positive and hopeful, or faulty and negative? Mine was wrought with mixed messages. My desires didn't match my experience.

I remember my grandma always wanting to lose those last five pounds. She wore girdles daily to hide her tummy and mentioned her struggle regularly. She just didn't seem free in her body. Similarly, my mom used to often only eat a mint chocolate Ayds square for lunch or "half of a half" of an English muffin. It was a phrase we giggled about, but the lack of freedom around food and body image at home was definitely noted. My sister shared that my dad once said, "If you didn't butter every square of your Eggo waffle, maybe your bum wouldn't be so big." As a teenager, that must have really hurt. Even my tall, handsome, slender brother said recently, "I hate it when I have anything extra around my midsection." (I can totally relate!) And I already mentioned the first nursery rhyme I remember my dad saying. The bottom line was that my family had hugely charged energy around food, weight, body image, and athleticism. So, my faulty belief system was, *I came from a long line of weight and image obsessed people who are never satisfied with their bodies and I can't be either.*

Even just reading those words today I can see the power they had over me for decades. Not only do we have to detox our environments, perhaps change our playmates, and take a look at our other addictions, we definitely have to challenge our thoughts around recovery. Is there something that needs to be cleaned up in this regard?

This was perhaps a heavy set of strategies, sweet reader. Please take heart. Go at your own pace implementing them. Reach out, and ask for the help you need to make these ideas a reality in your life. Your recovery will begin to take on a life of its own. Think of it as creating an entirely new body. Each step or idea is building new muscles. One might strengthen your arms, one your legs, one your core. Before you know it, you'll be a recovery Olympian. Just chip away at it. Aim for progress, not perfection.

Freedom Exercises

1. Go through each room of your house, and toss anything that triggers your eating disorder. This can include food items, photos of an ex-lover you miss terribly, clothing you've outgrown, distorted mirrors, or your scale.

2. List any habits that contribute to your eating disorder, and commit to creating new, positive, and opposing ones. Just stopping a habit won't work—a void will always want to be filled—so you need to fill it with something that will serve your recovery.

3. List your trigger places. Think about where you walk, drive, or meet people, and then list at least ten trigger places you will commit to avoiding.

4. List your trigger people. Commit to spending less or no time with them.

5. Join MeetUp.com or similar forum where you can begin to build solid relationships around recovery supportive activities.

6. Ask yourself if there are any other addictions that Source, Spirit, the Universe, God, or simply you, are asking you to quit as well? Notice those things, and become willing to release them.

7. Sit in a quiet place, and ponder your beliefs around recovery. See if any are faulty or conflicting. Notice if any subconscious ones come to the surface. Write them all down, challenge them mentally, and then transform each one into a belief that will better serve your recovery.

CHAPTER 6
FREEDOM STRATEGY 4: NURTURING YOUR BODY

"Let food be thy medicine and medicine be thy food."
—Hippocrates

Now let's talk about the elephant in the room—your body's nutritional needs. If you're anything like me, for years you haven't given a rat's ass about them. Your love of your size two skinny jeans far superseded the trivial matter of health. But what if I told you that nutritional deficiencies are the absolute precursor to the binge/purge cycle?

Facts About Weight Gain

This chapter may evoke fear. Even suggesting you eat certain foods can be triggering. The limiting belief? *I'm going to gain weight.* And your fear-based response? *No f*** way am I going to let that happen.*

The primary reason people remain trapped in the hell of bulimia is the fear of gaining weight if they quit. The number one reason! I know this to be true. I had (and frankly still do) the same unfounded fear. At the treatment center, one counselor asked me, "How much weight are you willing to gain to be free from bulimia?" *What the hell kind of question was that,* I thought? No, I'm going get over it *and* be skinny!

Interestingly, the statistics show most people of a healthy weight range who adopt regular eating habits and stop purging, end up only a few pounds heavier than their bulimic weight. Some even lose weight. Honestly, sweet sister, this is true. You will not balloon out. There may be temporary fluctuations, but once your body begins to trust in regular and nutritional feedings, it will normalize. Once you rehydrate and your body gets used to digesting food properly, the bloat will subside. Once your stunted metabolism revs up again, any unnecessary inches will come off.

Are you willing to put on a little weight to be healthy? It may be helpful to write down a number in case you begin to struggle. Keep reminding yourself how beautiful you are and that a few pounds either way will *not* make a difference! In fact, my husband fully prefers the new "rounder" me. Just a few years ago, that word would have given me major anxiety, but today it reminds me to be grateful for recovery. Shocking even to me, but true.

You're Starving

I heard someone say, "America is a nation of starving fat people." While it may sound oxymoronic and harsh, the reality is we have an obesity epidemic in North America, but many people are majorly malnourished. And other parts of the world are following suit. The thing is, obesity may reign, but nutritional deficiencies do as well. It's no wonder—fast foods, sugary foods, foods full of preservatives, and grain-laden foods—have become the norm. They have replaced the whole foods our ancestors ate, and we simply aren't getting the necessary nutrients for optimal health. Amazingly, even though we may be at a healthy weight or even over-weight, our bodies sense the nutritional deficiency and our survival instincts kick in. We desperately forage to bridge the gap. We layer meal upon meal upon meal, but we are never truly satiated.

On the other end of the spectrum, we starve ourselves. I'm guessing this is more your pattern. It was mine. While some funky food behaviors emerged as early as high school, I started really restricting food in college. Remember how powerful I felt if I limited myself to one muffin all day? And even more powerful if I didn't eat anything? Yeah, that. I starved myself. I remember looking around at my classmates eating their lunches—sandwiches, veggies, chips, whatever—and thinking I was such a freak. Why couldn't I just eat like other people? Or was I just destined for abnormality? I guessed so, so abnormality I embraced. Every study confirms that most bulimics or binge eaters started their journey into the land of a full-blown eating disorder by first restricting their food.

Do you get enough nutrients into your body on a regular basis? I don't mean that vegan dinner salad you eat every night. I mean regular and life-supporting nutrition. If not, this may be the very reason you can't walk away from the binge/purge cycle. You are working against hundreds of thousands of years of survival programing. Your body simply will not let you starve, so the binge switch flips on.

Re-feed Your Body

In order to flip the switch back to normalized eating, you will have to radically re-feed your body. This was my biggest challenge. Ironically, feeding yourself real nutrients will absolutely be the biggest beacon of light on your path to a full recovery from bulimia. It's so paradoxical. The very thing you don't want to do will be the catalyst to you recovering from your eating disorder. You need to eat. And I don't mean your favorite binge foods. I mean real nutrition. What you fear is what you must face courageously. Your Achilles heel—eating—will eventually be your super power. This is the part you will simply have to lovingly wrestle through. Feeding your body healthy foods and keeping them down will feel impossible, but it's mandatory.

For me, eating even one small and healthy item while alone would have inevitably led to a binge, which would have led to a purge. I just didn't have an off switch. At that time, I didn't really understand the importance of loading my system with nutrients, so I basically white-knuckled it and fought the primal urges as best I could despite the fact that my body was sending starvation signals to my brain. I'm thankful for the knowledge I've gained in the last handful of years. I'm no longer nutritionally starving myself, so I'm no longer fighting those robotic urges to binge.

This part of the program will take courage, planning, diligence, and a mentor or friend for support, but it is vital to your recovery. If you would like to quiet that screaming voice within that yells at you to binge, your body has to feel safe and supported. It has to know you will feed it regularly. It has to know you are living in abundance and not in scarcity. You will simply always be fighting those urges if you are not nutritionally satiated.

In short, I would love for you to add green smoothies, lean protein, fresh veggies, healthy fats, and eight large glasses of spring water to your daily intake. This will dramatically decrease your binge urges. I also recommend you avoid sugar, simple carbohydrates, grains, and alcohol as none of these items are nutritionally supportive. Eating on a fairly set schedule each day with no more than three hours between meals or snacks will also be helpful. This will signal your body that food is coming regularly and there is no need to binge now or hold onto more energy in the form of fat.

Here are some tips on re-feeding your body. The first five are foods to increase, and the rest are foods to avoid.

Green Smoothies

I'm such a fan of these alkalizing, nutritionally packed, yummy, and easy to make drinks. You will find it hard to sit and eat the amount of veggies that you can simply blend and drink. This can be the foundation for re-feeding your body so it will stop screaming at you for the wrong foods. Play with the recipe, but here is mine:

In a Blendtec, Vitamix, or other powerful blender put the following (and in this order for ease of blending):

- 1 large handful of ice
- About a thumb of peeled fresh ginger
- About a 1/2 a thumb of peeled fresh turmeric
- 2 stalks organic celery, cut into chunks
- 1/2 small organic cucumber, cut into chunks
- 1 small or 1/2 a large avocado
- Juice of half a lemon
- 1 raw egg (organic, free-range) if you have trouble getting enough protein
- Vanilla or lemon stevia drops to taste
- 1 large pinch of Himalayan sea salt
- 1 large handful of spinach
- Fresh spring water

Use the handful of spinach to push everything down into the blender. Then add enough water so your smoothie is the consistency you prefer—about one cup works well. Start with the blender on low for a few seconds to get things rolling, and then crank it up to high. Let it blend for 30 seconds. This will make quite an amount, but there is a lot of liquid considering both the water and the ice cubes, so don't be afraid to drink it all. The fiber from the veggies, the fat from the avocado, and the protein from the egg will physically satiate you until lunchtime, and the nutrient load will help satiate your eating disorder as well. You are literally feeding your freedom from bulimia with this drink.

Note: you have likely binged on a lot of sweet, sugary foods and your taste buds have adapted, so the green smoothie will taste bitter at first. But the few drops of vanilla stevia will help. Or, while you never want to have smoothies full of fruit—these will set you up for a sugar high/crash/possible binge—you can substitute the avocado for a banana to get a similar creamy consistency. Once your taste buds start to adjust to the green drink, slowly wean off the banana and use only the avocado to create a smooth, low-glycemic, tasty, power-packed drink. You can also try adding a teaspoon or tablespoon of coconut oil. I know. I know. Add more fat? Yikes! But trust me, it will signal your body that you are full which will start reducing your urge to binge. You may have to resist purging this drink at first—it's a lot of nutrition, and the full feeling may be triggering. If this is the case, please call your coach or friend for support.

Lean Protein
This is another building block to good health and one I really didn't like eating. I was vegetarian for many years in my 20s. *Save the animals* kind of thinking. Even after reintroducing meat into my diet, I didn't enjoy eating a lot of it, so high quality vegan protein powders became my go-to substitute. But they catered far too much to my sweet tooth. Rather than a healthy dinner of veggies, salad, and a lean protein, I would often have my standard wild organic blueberries, protein powder, seeds, nuts, cacao nibs, kefir, coconut oil, and coconut water.

All stirred up into a yummy treat. If I had a dollar for every time I had that meal, I'd be rich.

As we touched on in Chapter 2, variety is one of the basic human needs, so eating the same thing over and over and over again was not serving my mind or my body. Even after recovering from bulimia, I think the need for sweet flavors kept me in a less-than-body-loving cycle. I would opt for a chocolate croissant and a cappuccino for lunch rather than a health-supportive salad with boiled eggs or chicken. I cognitively knew which one served my body better, but my taste buds, and likely low dopamine and serotonin levels, would scream way louder than any healthy cognition. Those old habits were hard to change. I love that it's a *process* of recovery, not an *instant* of recovery. How do you feel about adding some healthy proteins into your diet? If you're willing, opt for free-range organic eggs, wild-caught fish, and grass-fed beef where possible, and avoid feedlot meats and any with added growth hormones, antibiotics, sugar or preservatives.

Fresh Organic Vegetables

I don't need to share much on this. You already know that veggies are the foundation for good health. And the more you feed your body high-quality nutrients, the less it will scream for a binge. Think of each salad, carrot, or Brussels sprout as feeding your recovery. Think of each celery stalk, asparagus spear, or snow pea as starving your bulimia. Each time you eat healthy, organic, vegetables, your body comes closer to a place of health and restoration, and your bulimia recedes further from your reality.

Healthy Fats

It has long been debunked that fats are the enemy. Research confirms repeatedly that healthy fats are mandatory for our body's homeostasis. It's fascinating to me that the obesity epidemic soared in America after the no- or low-fat craze hit. Do you know why? Food has to taste good. So when fat was removed from many processed items, it was replaced with sugar. No problem, right? A calorie is a calorie, and sugar has fewer of those than fat, yes? Wrong. Removing the fat removed the very thing that triggers your body's satiety. Have you ever wondered why you could eat two or three low-fat muffins without wanting to stop, but after one full-fat muffin, you were satisfied? Not only does fat signal satiety, the extra sugar in the non-fat varieties signals your body to eat more. It's a primal instinct. Sweet foods were rare for our ancestors, so if they did come across a berry bush or a fig tree, eating just one would signal to their brains, *Yes! Jackpot! Eat as much as you can. You never know when you will get this again!* We were programmed to gain weight for survival. And sweets are the perfect mechanism. Interestingly, fats do the opposite. They signal we have had enough, and they promote weight loss.

I started (reluctantly) experimenting with adding two teaspoons of coconut oil to my matcha tea in the mornings. I was so afraid it would make me fat, but I was willing to feed my body what it needed. Surprisingly, I didn't gain an ounce. And believe me, I added up the extra daily calories and multiplied it by 365. I'm still a bit neurotic like that. It was a hefty annual increase, but there was no bodily effect. In fact, when people start this protocol, they often release weight as it curbs their appetite throughout the morning. Ken's parents collectively lost 30 pounds within a few months when they started blending fat into their morning coffee! The old paradigm, "A calorie is a calorie is a calorie," is no longer valid. It's how we metabolize each calorie that's important. Your body yearns for healthy fats, so do it a favor and provide them.

You might also consider adding some healthy Omega-3 oil to your daily intake. This will do wonders for your skin, hair, and nails. Omega-3s also balance hormones, even our mood fluctuations, and decrease certain food cravings. Simply taking a Norwegian-sourced fish oil or krill oil supplement and pouring a tablespoon of flax seed oil on your salad will provide you with the necessary daily Omega-3s to optimize your health.

Water

One type of hunger, as mentioned in Chapter 2, has nothing to do with food—it has to do with hydration. Make sure you get plenty of water throughout the day, and then drink some more. It's best to even measure out a few liters in the morning and pour it into containers you love drinking from. You'll be surprised at how hard it is at first to get in your daily ration. If you're chronically dehydrated, as most bulimics are, you are like a dry sponge. Have you ever tried to wipe the counter with a dry sponge? Not very effective, right? You might find the water passes right through you quite quickly at first, but as your cells begin to absorb the fluids, you'll need fewer visits to the restroom, and your cells will be happier.

Hydrating in this way may cause you to gain a pound or two at first, depending on your level of dehydration. Please drink anyway. You will release some of the excess water as your bodily systems get accustomed to being consistently hydrated. The best source is natural spring water, then reverse osmosis water, and the absolute last resource is tap water. It is usually filled with chlorine and fluoride—both disruptive to your health.

Sugar

Avoid sugar as it can easily trigger a binge. Again, millennia of survival conditioning will ensure this. We were designed to crave calorie dense foods, but they were previously scarce. Our DNA has not caught up to the level of food abundance we experience in many parts of the world today. If you really want something sweet, choose foods sweetened with stevia or raw organic honey. Stevia has no glycemic load (although it can alter your insulin sensitivity), and raw honey has beneficial vitamins, enzymes, phytonutrients and other nutritional elements. Avoid refined sugar, as it is basically poison to your system and ultimately toxic to your mind.

Simple carbohydrates

Sugar is not the only simple carb to avoid—keep rice, potatoes, grains, and wheat products to a minimum as well. They essentially turn into sugar once digested. Many studies indicate humans were just not meant to eat grains, period. Complex carbohydrates are much more supportive to your recovery as they help keep your blood sugar levels consistent. If you think you can't live without bread, rice, and pasta, think again! There are so many alternatives available. You can use veggies like spaghetti squash or zucchini pasta under your favorite marinara sauce, cauliflower rice for paella, or Paleo bread made from almond or coconut flour for your morning toast.

Alcohol

Alcohol is full of empty calories and sugars. It also lowers your ability to resist temptation so you may find yourself eating all sorts of foods you would otherwise avoid. This could set you up for a relapse. If you really want a few cocktails with friends, no problem, just be wise about it. Opt for club soda-based drinks with perhaps muddled herbs rather than the sugary sweet version like daiquiris or margaritas. My favorite choice is Hendrick's gin, Perrier, muddled mint, cucumber, and lime. It's refreshing, and doesn't steer me into a sugar coma.

Supplementation to Ease the Urge

Dr. Daniel Amen, New York Times Best Selling Author of *Change Your Brain, Change Your Life,* describes those with bulimia as a Type 3 Addict, meaning we are both compulsive *and* impulsive. Compulsive addicts have trouble shifting attention off the object of desire—food, the Internet, gambling, sex—and have trouble seeing other options when faced with a decision. Brain scans show this is mostly due to low serotonin levels. Impulsive addicts obviously have trouble with impulse control. We say we won't do the behavior, but can't resist when faced with it. Brain scans show this is a result of low activity in the prefrontal cortex, likely caused by low levels of dopamine. This impairs judgment, impulse control, planning, and follow-through. We can become distracted, bored, inattentive, and impulsive. ADD anyone?

We bulimics have a double whammy to deal with—impulsive and compulsive control issues. But supplementation can work wonders. This topic could take up an entire book so you might like to research it on your own, but Dr. Amen suggests at least these few simple hacks: to raise levels of serotonin, supplement with 5-HTP and to raise your dopamine levels, try adding green tea or L-tyrosine to your diet.

Most people with eating disorders are also deficient in vitamin D3, omega-3 fats, vitamin K2, magnesium, potassium, folate, vitamin B12, vitamin E, vitamin A, iodine, calcium, and iron, so adding these nutrients will also help your body repair. Supplementation will also ease your nutritional hunger which will help the urges to binge subside.

Movement as Medicine

As you begin to love yourself with your food choices, you will naturally begin to love yourself with your exercise program. This took me so long to realize.

A few years into abstinence I started realizing that my exercise habits were part of my eating disorder. For a few decades, I unknowingly used running as a bulimic outlet. (Bulimia can be anything we use to rid ourselves of excess calories—exercise, purging, laxatives, diuretics, or periods of fasting.) I would lace up my Nikes and head out on the seawall. Five or six miles would tire me out enough to ease the mental tension and rid myself of any excess fat floating around my midsection. Block after block, mile after mile, I ran. Often, I wished I could run off the edge of the planet and be done with it. Peace and ease were elusive feelings. Interestingly, people positively reinforced my frenzy. "You've already run 10K and it's only 7am?" Or, "Wow, you're so fit—look at those leg muscles! I want to be disciplined like you." If they only knew my motive for running excessively was so ignoble—to get out of my freaky mind—they may not have been so generous with their praise. I felt like such a fraud. This is not the movement as medicine I'm referring to.

As more time passes between my last binge/purge and the present, I have found my movement choices have become much more gentle and spiritual. I traded CrossFit for kundalini, boot camps for ashtanga, long distance running for hiking, and TRX for vinyasa. It's a wholesale change.

Pre-abstinence, the energy behind my exercise choices was quite frenetic and self-punishing. While I find things like CrossFit and boot camps super fun, essentially I was beating my body into some sort of shape I thought was attractive—stronger, trimmer, and more toned. But did I leave each session a better person? Maybe physically and even mentally, but not emotionally or spiritually. It became insufficient. If I was going to spend time exercising, there had to be a spiritual component also. Not to say that *anything* we do can't have a spiritual component if we declare it as such, but I was looking for something inherently spiritual. I found that in yoga.

While I had practiced yoga in my 20s, my mind was way too squirrely to spend 60 to 90 minutes on a two-foot by six-foot mat. It was torture. But as my monkey mind began to abate, that mat became my friend. As my body became more flexible and fluid, so did my mind. As my mind opened up, so did my spirit. Yoga is a win-win-win and a powerful piece of the addiction-healing puzzle. Tommy Rosen, best selling author of *Recovery 2.0,* uses kundalini and other forms of yoga to gain access to the extraordinary healing power already within each of us. Yoga is a foundational part of the global recovery work he spearheads, and I couldn't agree with him more.

The Healing Power of Sleep

One of the easiest ways to care for your body in recovery is to get enough sleep. Gone are the days of A-type personalities wearing their "I only need four to five hours of sleep per night" badges of honor. Countless studies now indicate that the vast majority of people require at least seven to eight hours of sleep for optimal health. A-typers are even catching on. It seems the badge of honor is now "I'm smart, informed, and know that sleep is vital to performance, so I get at least seven hours." It's amazing how the cultural view around sleep has changed.

Have you ever noticed your bulimic urges are much harder to resist when you're tired? Mine were. The familiar acronym HALT is valid and effective. When faced with a perceived need to eat, halt and ask, "Am I **H**ungry, **A**ngry, **L**onely, or **T**ired?" If you're not truly hungry, emotional eating will likely fall into one of the three latter categories. So never let yourself get over-tired. It will serve your recovery well.

Here are a few simple strategies to increase your chance of getting a good night's sleep:

- Decrease water intake a few hours before bed
- Make sure your bedroom is quiet (silicone earplugs come in handy)
- Keep your bedroom below 70 degrees
- Remove all electronics, including the TV, from your bedroom
- Stop using technology 90 minutes before retiring

- Get to bed at or before 10pm—the value of sleep between 10pm and 2am is reportedly optimal
- Prepare for bed one hour before you actually want to be asleep— you are a woman—your route to the pillow is always circuitous
- Keep your bedroom as dark as possible (I use an eye guard—my poor husband!)

Getting a good night's rest is like picking low-hanging fruit to fill your recovery basket. These sleep strategies can be invaluable in helping reduce your binge/purge impulses.

What if I Just Can't Stop Eating?

That's a good question and one I asked myself repeatedly in early recovery. After a few decades of not being able to stop, what gives now? The answer? Commitment, nutrition, and support.

If you are still reading this book, you are likely very committed. You have reached a time in your life where you are tired of settling. You are tired of watching others self-actualize while you are stuck in your little life ruled by bulimia. You are ready for an upgrade. You can check **commitment** off the list.

The next step will be re-feeding yourself. This is a significant key. It's the combination to a vault you have not yet been able to open. I can't stress it enough. You will fight a never-ending battle if you keep starving your body of the **nutrition** it needs for survival and thrival (you won't find that word in the dictionary!) The more your body trusts you to feed it properly, the less it will scream at you to feed it everything in sight. And it *will* signal you to stop eating. I promise you. I never thought that would happen for me. I honestly thought I missed that gene—the one that tells you to stop stuffing your face. But once I fed myself proper nutrition my urges subsided, my willpower emerged, and homeostasis was established.

The last piece of this part of the puzzle is **support**. You likely didn't have a strong support network in place before, so of course you kept falling back into bulimia. But you know better now. Perhaps you have a few names and numbers from your EDA group, and maybe you have reached out to a few other safe souls. Maybe you and I have even connected. Acknowledge to yourself that you are on the road to recovery. The vital thing at this stage is actually *using* the support that has come into your life. This is not a time for pride or self-sufficiency. It's time to call in the troops.

I remember one humbling weekend during my first round of recovery in the late 1990s. I had been doing well all week, but felt the binge/purge cycle coming on. I just knew I could not be home alone all weekend and stay abstinent. So I uncharacteristically picked up the phone and asked one of my mentors, Cathy V, if I could please come and stay at her house for the weekend. Looking back, it was perhaps a lot to ask—she had two kids, a dog, a husband, and a busy life—but she accepted without hesitation. When you are ready to help yourself, people will scramble to help you, too. Create and lean on your support systems. There will be plenty of time in full recovery where you will be able to reciprocate.

Freedom Exercises

1. Make a shopping list including the green smoothie ingredients.
2. If grocery stores are triggering, call your sponsor or trusted friend, and ask her to go shopping with you.
3. Commit to feeding your body three green smoothies this week. Give yourself some sort of reward for completing this assignment. Then consider doing the same the following week. Ideally you'll work your way up to a green smoothie everyday.

4. Write down five different types of exercises you absolutely love and you know for certain are not feeding your eating disorder. Only you will know. What fed mine may starve yours. And vice versa. Create and commit to a weekly exercise program including one or all of these forms of movement.

CHAPTER 7

FREEDOM STRATEGY 5:
WEANING OFF BEHAVIORS

"The simple intention to surrender control
is all you need to experience miracles."
—**Gabrielle Bernstein**, *The Universe Has Your Back*

I f you've committed to re-feeding and re-hydrating your body, as
well as making many of the necessary daily changes to support your
recovery, it's time to start thinking about weaning yourself from the
binge/purge cycle. Gulp. Yes, it's time. Are you ready? Even if you have
just an ounce of willingness, you're on the right track. Recovery is a
journey. Be gentle but firm with yourself during this stage.

To support the weaning process, it will be helpful to get in touch
with what bulimia is providing for you and what it is costing you.

Often the pain of staying the same has to be more acute than the pain of changing for us to take action. Doing a cost/benefit analysis and seeing it in black and white can help amp up the staying-the-same pain meter. In your recovery journal, list all the things you get from your eating disorder. Be brutally honest. No one will see this list except you. Then list the costs. How is your eating disorder holding you back from upgrading your life? Be gentle with yourself here. Remember, there have been valid reasons for your behaviors. Most importantly, remind yourself that you are on the path to freedom. Try to have no regrets, just hope. You have used your eating disorder as a survival tactic, and it has worked so far. But it's losing its efficacy, yes? It's getting increasingly costly rather than beneficial.

Really ponder your list. Let it sink into your heart. Allow the price of your bulimia to penetrate to such a degree that you begin to see its devastating, life draining lies. Moments during the weaning process will seem excruciating—these are the times to pull out your list. Ask yourself, *Is bulimia really worth giving up all these things?*

It's a Numbers Game

While my self-discipline was amazing in areas like work, exercise, my home life, and creative endeavors, I could not self-modulate my eating. When food was involved, I regressed to childhood. Actually, worse than childhood—children have a natural shut off switch, which I sorely lacked. No matter how many thousands (literally) of days I said to myself, *I will NOT act out today,* I couldn't stop. This is where the numbers game came into play.

As mentioned earlier, under Cesar's care I was able to wean off bulimic behaviors within a handful of months. But I didn't mention the details. Around our fifth week of counseling, he asked me if I was willing to start letting go of bulimia. My thinking went something like, *Holy s***, really? Are we there already? Can't we ruminate about feelings,* *the past, the present, the future for just a little while longer? Are we really going to get serious about recovery? I just want to be skinny for a few more months.* I still believed recovery meant I would be shopping in plus-size boutiques. But I was willing, so I said yes.

At the time, I was acting out seven days a week including many multiple times per day, so Cesar asked me if I could commit to having just one day free from bulimia that week. One full day seemed quite impossible, but I had to start somewhere, and these baby steps set me up for success. This became our game, and I did not want to show up to my next appointment having failed. The following week, I marched into his office knowing I would get a gold star. It dawned on me during that process how attached I was to external validation. Accolades from others had become more rewarding than abiding in my own inner sense of worthiness. Not surprising since, at that point, I had very little self-esteem. My value was wrapped up in what I did, not in who I was as a human being. Knowing what I did in private stripped away all sense of internal value. I literally needed the approval and validation from others just to feel neutral.

After learning to crawl with one free day, we began trying to walk, then to run—playing with formulas like six days per week and only three of those days could have multiples, to six days a week with no multiples, to five days a week with two multiples and so on. I remember when we got down to only once per week—it was a miracle milestone. And I knew what was coming. Full abstinence.

In case that all sounds so neat and clean and easy and formulaic, I want to lovingly warn you it might not feel that way during the process. While writing about this phase of recovery, I became curious about what I was really feeling at the time. A journal entry dated February 4th, 2013—two months or so into the weaning off phase—said it all.

Wow. Tormented. For the last few weeks I have been in constant torture. My mind will not stop. The only thing that shuts it up is Ed. I feel so chunky.

So out of control. So scared. So disempowered. WTF is going on with me?
Can't stand Ed—f*** you!! I am amazing. I choose health. I choose sanity.
I choose to say no to foods when I know they don't serve my highest self. I've
got this. XO

I share this to let you know you are not alone in your thoughts. I
literally believed I would never overcome my eating disorder and, even if
by some miracle I did, that my mind would torment me forever. Either
way, the future felt dismal. But those were all lies perpetuated by bulimia.
Once I released them, I was able to transform my disempowering
thoughts into empowering ones. You will be able to as well.

Thoughts Fuel Your Actions

One last thought on thoughts—do you agree that thoughts fuel your
actions? I do, and I think they fuel even more than our actions. In
his famous quote, Mahatma Gandhi says, "Your beliefs become your
thoughts, your thoughts become your words, your words become your
actions, your actions become your habits, your habits become your
values, your values become your destiny." Powerful. Your thoughts will
eventually either diminish or upgrade your life. They will keep you from
your destiny or usher you powerfully into it.

When I think back to the barrage of negativity my brain had to deal
with, it's no wonder I needed to drown it out with various addictions.
Thoughts can stem from early childhood trauma, being bullied in grade
school, middle school sexual abuse, rejection in adulthood, or all of the
above. How they entered, is less consequential. It's what we do with
them that is important.

During the weaning process, you will deal with two primary types
of disempowered thinking—real feelings you need to honor, accept, and
then challenge so your resulting actions are in line with your values, and
then false thoughts you need to flat out refute.

The real ones might be something like, *I feel fat so I want to hibernate tonight.* Other than the fact that fat is not a feeling (if you dig, the underling feelings are usually more like fear, sadness, or anxiety), it might be how you truly feel. In the moment, it is real. So you can lovingly honor the feeling and then challenge yourself to a thought that would serve your life better. *I feel fat and I'm going to the party anyway.* It honors and validates your thoughts and then steers your actions in a healthy way. The point is to create a new conversation and cast a new vision based on your values, not your thoughts. Do you value connection with people? Then honor that you feel scared about going out in public, but do it anyway. Serve your higher self by changing your thoughts. Do your thoughts shout, *do not get in that pool with your kids, you need to lose weight first!?* But you value family fun time and connection? Lovingly acknowledge the feeling, and move towards your values anyway.

Other types of thoughts you might battle are downright lies. And those you can handle entirely differently. This will take a concentrated effort, as during the weaning stage they will likely become incredibly acute. This barrage of thoughts will send you running back to your bulimia if you're not diligent. Conversely, if you take some time to really think about what goes on between your ears and ponder how those thoughts affect your actions, you'll start to gain ground. The volume—both in number and decibel level—of negative thoughts will decrease, and self-love with start to flow freely.

Here is another excerpt from my journal dated January 19, 2013—right in the height of weaning off of bulimia. Hopefully seeing my thoughts will have you feel less alone in yours and will spurn an honest probing into what thoughts you think on a regular basis. With awareness comes the ability to challenge them.

Top Ten Negative Thoughts (& The Actual Truth)

1. *I've wasted my life. (I've had an amazing life and have so much more to live!)*
2. *I'll never tap into my full potential. (I'm always growing toward my potential.)*
3. *My body has lost its muscle tone as I've aged. (My body is beautiful and capable of taking me on many athletic adventures.)*
4. *I'm a terrible wife. (Ken said he couldn't have even invented a more perfect wife for him.)*
5. *I'm a bad friend, aunt, sis-in-law, sister. (I'm a loving, loyal, trusted friend, aunt, sis-in-law, sister.)*
6. *I have no ability to succeed. (I have all I need to succeed!)*
7. *I will always struggle with Ed. (My struggle with Ed is coming to an end!)*
8. *If people knew me, they would reject me. (When people know me fully, they embrace me fully!)*
9. *I'm not lovable. (I am love personified.)*
10. *My thighs, ass, and waist are chunky monkey. (My thighs, ass, and waist are gorgeous and take me to my dreams!)*

Can you see how sinister thoughts can be? And how simple they are to transform. The more you practice, the more your subconscious mind will start tapping into the truth. It will recognize the fleeting negativity and remind you to flip it to positivity. Are your thoughts similar to mine above? Would you think these negative thoughts about anyone else? Me neither. So why do we allow our eating disordered minds to think these thoughts about ourselves? Let's not.

Tools to Stop Binging

You've likely researched recovery extensively in your quest for abstinence and will know about many of the following tools, but I would be remiss if I didn't at least briefly touch on them. The trick is actually *using* them. I was terrible at that before I got serious about recovery. I had a full-blown tool belt full of the best quality gadgets. I'd accumulated them over two decades, but they were just too heavy to pick up in the face of a bulimic episode. That changed when I flicked the switch from unwillingness to willingness—I went from being a little weakling with spaghetti string arms to a powerful Olympian. The weight of the tools was all in my head. I just had to begin using them.

Below is a list of practices you can implement to either decrease the urge to binge in the very moment or to decrease the number of binges coming on in the first place. There are hundreds of tools to distract or relax you, so in time you can develop a list of your own. For now, here are some that worked for me. I hope you find them helpful.

1. **Flee temptation!** If the food in your fridge or cupboards is calling you, get out of the house, and do *not* bring money. If you have work to do, go to the library or some other safe place. Ed is tricky, and you'll have to outsmart it. I can't tell you how many times I did the right thing by leaving the house only to find myself buying binge foods ten minutes later. But no money = no food. Be smarter than Ed.

2. **Call your sponsor or trusted friend.** Please give up your independence, even if just for a while. You need people deeply in this stage of recovery. You need people in every stage, but particularly in this one. I found that most people are desperate for true and honest connections in this crazy digital world and are therefore delighted to be your confidant.

3. **Go for a walk.** There's nothing like the endorphins created by exercising in nature to help ease the urge. Set your watch for 30 minutes, and just get out there. No questions, no thinking, just action.

4. **Journal.** This was an invaluable tool for me, and I think it will be for you too. Your eating disorder is trying to get real needs met in harmful ways. Writing can connect you with that cut-off part of yourself and can bring it into the light. Your unmet needs start to be exposed. Explore your feelings, your longings, the things missing in your life. Notice your negative thinking and write the opposite, as in the example above. Just explore. This distraction can be the difference between a massive breakthrough in self-discovery and healing or simply acting out in another useless binge/purge session.

5. **Draw a hot Epsom salt bath.** Then light some candles, grab a book or magazine, and treat yourself to some beautiful nurturing down time. It will soothe your soul. The magnesium will even help with any mineral deficiencies your bulimia has likely caused.

6. **Hit the mat.** Yoga is the spiritual movement and medicine my internal doctor ordered. I started yoga in my early 20s, but could never stick to it—I was just too squirrelly. But as recovery became increasingly solid, the mat no longer felt like a torture chamber. It was no longer claustrophobic. It had become a lifeline I will use for a lifetime. You might want to add it to your tool kit, too.

7. **Get consistent sleep.** Did you ever notice your resolve is much lower when you're tired? As mentioned earlier, studies indicate most people's optimum number is seven to eight hours each night. Do what it takes to give yourself that gift.

8. **Eat consistent, small, nutritious meals only when hungry.** If you never get ravenous, the likelihood of a binge/purge session diminishes. And if you are nutritionally satisfied, your body is less likely to scream for food when you aren't physically hungry. To help keep portions smaller, use smaller plates—the standard

American dinner plates have become huge. And before even putting something on your plate, ask yourself, *is this a recovery supporter or a recovery saboteur.* Then act accordingly. Only you will truly know what works for you. Lastly, only eat when you're hungry. It may seem obvious, but sometimes the best food choice is no food at all.

9. **Do your favorite hobby.** During my first stab at recovery in the late 1990s, I loved sewing quilts. Something about all the colors and textures and design possibilities was intoxicating. I loved creating something beautiful out of nothing. I wound up teaching classes on various techniques, and it became my passion. This was the perfect recovery hobby. It was soul nurturing, and it kept my hands busy. Stuffing my face and sewing were mutually exclusive activities –I only have one pair of hands. Find a hobby that will support your recovery, and dive in.

10 **Throw away left over food.** Then pour water, coffee grinds, or anything on it that will make it repulsive. I'm not joking. Do whatever it takes to avoid a binge. If you can avoid the binge, you can avoid the purge.

11. **Pray and meditate.** This step came later down the process for me. It seemed as though at first I had to conquer unhealthy action with healthy action. Just sitting in one place in prayer and meditation would last all of 20 seconds before my squirrely mind had me up and running toward the fridge. Anything to ease the angst. But as I logged more and more free days, I was able to actually do the practice that has been prescribed for millennia. I'm not saying you can't be praying and meditating as you go about your active day, but the prayer and meditation I'm suggesting here is a quiet, intentional, focused connection with your Source. *Be still.* Why? So you can connect with your

true identity, your worth, your amazingness. Being totally available to not only transmit your thoughts and heart, but also to receiving Source's highest thoughts and intentions for you. There are countless forms of quiet meditation. Just find one that works for you.

12. **Lastly, if you sense a binge/purge coming on, again, HALT!** Ask yourself, *Am I Hungry, Angry, Lonely or Tired?* Then choose to address the need in a healthy way.

Remember, the more you use any of these tools and the more you resist the urge to binge, the more you will create new habits, combat your reward sensitivity, and create new neural pathways. The old channels were creating a seemingly insatiable desire to binge. The new ones will bring you recovery.

Tools to Stop Purging

Many of the strategies listed above will automatically take care of the purging. In the height of my bulimia, if there was no binge, there was no purge as purging was useless unless it was voluminous. But as I started decreasing my binge/purge episodes and my body weight went up a few pounds, I did have to proactively fight the urge to purge, even after a normal meal. Here are some tools I hope will help you as you fight these urges as well. Many are similar as the tools for reducing the urge to binge.

1. **Flee temptation!** Again, this is key. You may need to plan ahead. If you're going to a dinner party and are afraid of purging when you get home, ask a friend if you can stay the night at her house. I kid you not. When I did this, I always felt totally freakish, but my friends loved that I felt close enough to ask. And my soul got a big win when I woke up the next day still abstinent.

2. **Call your sponsor or trusted friend.** Pick up the phone, and tell her you're getting the urge and need her to walk you off the ledge.

3. **Go for a walk.** Allow yourself 30-60 minutes for your stomach to digest before returning home.

4. **Journal.** This can be the best tool for bringing a breakthrough. Sitting with a full stomach and the desperate urge to get rid of it will bring up so many deep emotions and thoughts. Stay with them. The one meal in your belly will not alter anything on your body. But the deep processing work you do in the meantime could have massive positive consequences for your mind and your recovery.

5. **Take a nap.** You cannot purge and sleep simultaneously.

6. **Lose yourself in your favorite recovery supportive hobby.** Just keeping your hands and mind busy will help you ride the wave right into abstinence.

7. **Research a trip.** Think of one you've always wanted to take and then get lost in the joy of planning it. You don't need to necessarily book it—just having fun researching will help take your mind off your urges.

8. **Clean out a drawer or cupboard.** This is one of my favorites. It keeps you distracted, it keeps your hands busy, and it provides instant gratification.

9. **Google the effects of purging on your system.** Learn the gory details. Stare it down. Take your power back with information. Not that you want your recovery to be fear based, but learning how purging negatively impacts your body can be enough of a deterrent in that moment of stress to get you through the urge.

10. **Pray and meditate.** Anytime you connect with your Source, you will be filled with a greater sense of peace, purpose, and power. If you can commit to holding off the urge to purge for

even ten minutes of prayer and meditation, it will likely subside in the presence of truth. If it doesn't, commit to another ten minutes. And another. And another. Until the urge has passed.

Those are the tools I used most frequently to wean off my binge/purge episodes. They are specific to the binge eating and vomiting cycle. If your purge of choice is laxatives or excess exercise, the tools can be easily tweaked to help you reduce your episodes as well. Slowly wean off each, decreasing by an agreed upon amount each week. In the case of laxative abuse, you may need a magnesium supplement or an herbal laxative to help get you off any harsh drug store varieties. The ideal is to quit them altogether, just as the ideal is to no longer vomit. You've got this.

Handling Relapse

There may be some who quit bulimia cold turkey and never go back. To those souls I say, "Holy crap! Amazing. Power to you!" And, "How the hell did you do that!?" But for the rest of us, for whom it is a two-steps forward and one-step back process, relapse is inevitable. So let's declare that up front and decide how to deal with it. Lord knows I have a lifetime of experience dealing with relapse and trust me, dealing with it is a highly complex and complicated procedure. It goes like this:

Get up, dust off your knees, and get back on the horse, every time.

That's obviously a tongue-in-cheek and simplistic answer. The longer answer is to use your intellect to figure out why the slip happened in the first place. Then create structures to mitigate your risk of it happening again in the future. This will build your character and ultimately your recovery.

One such structure was moving homes. It was a pretty drastic measure, but one I knew was necessary for me to successfully quit bulimia. I had lived on my own for most of my adult life and isolation was one of my major triggers. Whether it stemmed from the aloneness I felt as a child, from the unmet adult longing for a life-partner, or from the general sense that I didn't fit in very well in the world, I knew coming home to an empty place year in, year out, was not serving my recovery. So I got busy looking for a larger home and a roommate. I found the most adorable house in my same neighborhood and knew it was perfect. I signed the lease trusting my roommate would materialize. And she did. For the next number of years, Cheryl and I lived together, and her very presence was a structure that helped separate me from my bulimia, even if only for a season.

What are some of your common triggers, and what structures can you put into place to reduce their effect? They don't have to be that drastic. Remember the large tubs of movie popcorn that called to me? If I felt weak, I simply knew to avoid the movies. When I got stronger, my structure was to tell my movie companion that I will be tempted to buy popcorn, but do *not* let me. I often asked for the same support at dinnertime —please stop me if I go for a second helping, or don't let me order dessert. Having to ask your support people to be your food police may seem like very tenuous recovery, but this strategy is really only necessary in the early stages. Think of it like using a spotter at the gym. They support you as you bench press increasingly heavy weights in case you weaken and drop one on your face. That would not be fun. But as you workout, you gain strength and no longer need them for the lighter lifts. Movie popcorn seemed like a 250-pound weight at one point, but it became a 5-pounder I can throw around with ease as I gained solid recovery muscles.

This is your journey. Only you will know your triggers. It's important you ponder them, write them down, and devise a plan on dealing with them using counteracting structures. Be prepared so you can eventually be free.

Measuring Your Progress

Measuring progress in terms of days abstinent is a topic on which people in the eating disorder recovery world disagree. Do we count the days since our last binge/purge like they advocate in Alcohol and Narcotics Anonymous? Or do we look for more subjective signs of progress? The differing opinions stem from the fact that an alcoholic or drug user can definitively say that such and such a date was the last time she used, but someone with an eating disorder can't exactly. Firstly, we need to use food multiple times daily for our very survival. Secondly, can we *really* say that second helping of dinner wasn't a binge? Or that the extra mile we ran wasn't a purge? Can we really say it *was*? Food and exercise behaviors can be pretty subjective. These nuances cause opinions to vary. So I will just give you my view and why it was crucial for me to have a recovery date. This is not truth—it's just my view. Tracking abstinence was wildly empowering. And abstinence meant I did not throw up my food. I kept it simple. No purge = no bulimia.

While the purge rule was hard and unbending, I was super gentle with myself as I weaned off binging—if I overate slightly and then stopped, I actually considered it more of a win than if I had just eaten normally. To pull myself off the ledge of a binge took Herculean strength in those days. To just sit with a full stomach and process the incredible anxiety it produced was a victory. I counted it as a massive plume in the cap of my recovery. Measuring progress in terms of days abstinent became an empowering tool. Every May 9th, I am reminded of how far I've come. My husband and I celebrate that day like we would a birthday. Actually even more so. I didn't do anything to be born, but I had to work my ass off to quit bulimia. So you decide. If it serves you, have a recovery day. It will be a moving target at first. I had a handful of dates I thought would be it in the weeks and months leading up to May 9th, but that's okay. One eventually stuck.

If it triggers you to track hard dates, I still urge you to record your progress. Progress can come in so many packages! Are you obsessing less about food and your body? Are your episodes becoming less frequent or less intense? Are you able to stop what would have previously developed into a binge? Can you just sit with a full stomach and process the feelings? Can you be in environments that used to be massive triggers? Are you more peaceful? Asking these types of question and writing the answers in your recovery journal will be such a beautiful record of your journey. It's often the small things that point to the colossal progress you are making.

I'm happy you've had the courage to read this far. That shows your commitment to upgrading your life from one caught in the bulimic cycle to one walking toward your destiny. Be proud of yourself and take heart—weaning off behaviors is where the rubber hits the recovery road and where true freedom lies. Be sure to reach out for support during this tenuous stage.

FREEDOM EXERCISES

1. Review the cost benefit analysis you completed in this chapter. Really sit with the costs. Then imagine your upgraded life— life free from bulimia—and notice the stark contrast. Try to actually feel the feelings associated with your new life so your soul will want to live into them.

2. Play the numbers game—commit to giving up 10-15% of your bulimic episodes this week. Share this with your accountability person, and set a day and time you will report back to her.

3. Journal about what comes up for you as you wean off behaviors. What feelings begin to surface? What conversations are you being nudged to have? What actions are calling you to take?

4. As you have success each week, up the ante for the following week.

5. Write down your top ten disempowering thoughts and then the opposing ten positive truths.

6. Write down your binge and purge triggers, and decide how you will stand in the face of them during future temptations.

7. Record some of the progress you've made so far.

8. Pick up the tools in your tool kit. You've got this.

CHAPTER 8

FREEDOM STRATEGY 6: STRENGTHENING YOUR SOUL

"There is no greater gift you can give or receive than to honor your calling. It's why you were born. And how you become most alive."
—**Oprah Winfrey**

How are you doing so far? I know there is a lot to think about. Recovery is work. It's gritty. It's courageous. By even researching recovery, you've shown yourself you want this. You want to be well. So let's dig in further.

Thus far we've mainly addressed external changes—coming clean with another person, arming yourself with resources, re-feeding your body, detoxing your home, changing your habits and friends, and perhaps creating a whole new metaphorical Rat Park for yourself.

95

Now let's get clear on a mandatory aspect of long-term recovery—strengthening your soul.

When I look back on my bulimia, not only was my body starved and weak, my soul was, too. While my Rat Park was pretty awesome—I had an exciting life filled with an abundance of friends, family, travel, beautiful things, exciting experiences, pets, growth, and love—my soul was disconnected so I couldn't truly enjoy any of it. My external Rat Park didn't nurture me because my internal soul was starving. I normally left a social gathering or an amazing experience feeling empty rather than filled. I was disconnected from my Source. You know the feeling, yes? You are with your favorite people—laughing, giggling, sharing fun activities, reaching certain goals, enjoying life—but since your soul is not full, you are left ravenous, not refreshed.

You might have worked through strategies one through five to perfection, but if you don't take care of your very essence, you will likely relapse. Spirituality is like food—just as a wonderful meal nourishes the body, spiritually strengthens your soul. Likewise, some representations of spirituality you will love, others you won't. If a certain church, mosque, ashram, temple, or spiritual gathering place has piqued your interest, heed the call. If you've been drawn to African drumming or Native American sweat lodges or Transcendental Meditation, go check them out. Explore. If you don't like the spiritual flavor, don't finish the dish. Keep searching until you find your soul food. You may also find it helpful to create a spot in your home only for your soul's refreshment. Include an alter, candles, a mediation pillow, pictures of your spiritual leaders, or whatever else helps ground you and connect you with your Source. Go there often when your soul needs sustenance. Addiction recovery is an intensely spiritual journey, and I encourage you to dig deeply—both out in the world and into your very essence.

Your Bulimia's Purpose

Now is a great time to get honest about the purpose behind your bulimia. I'm convinced we humans are wildly smart, hell bent on survival, and don't do things repeatedly that don't serve us in some capacity. Before you can let go of your eating disorder for good and reconnect with your soul, it's imperative you become aware of its underlying purpose. I wrote the following journal entry as I was getting close to quitting bulimia. I didn't know it at the time, but it was just a few short months before my final episode.

What I love about my Ed and will need to grieve in recovery:
- *Stress relief*
- *Can eat "forbidden foods" with no weight gain*
- *Sense of control*
- *Sense of peace*
- *An escape from reality*
- *Don't have to grow up*
- *Something to obsess about and focus on so the rest of the mind goes quiet*
- *Skinny jeans!*

I'm happy to get rid of my Ed as it has robbed me of:
- *Meaningful relationships*
- *Heart connection*
- *A healthy internal system*
- *Nice glowing skin*
- *Peace of mind*
- *Power*
- *Happiness*
- *Success in my projects*

- *Time*
- *Connection from reality and people*
- *Countless thousands of dollars*
- *Being a mama*

It's a pretty sobering list. Once I put it down in black and white, I could see the scales were tipped extremely in one direction. My Ed was taking far more than it was giving. Once I saw that, I was able to relax my grip. It also became clear that my bulimia was all about fear—fear of the past, present, and future. Fear of situations. Fear of people. Fear of myself. I realized that everything I wanted in life couldn't exist in the face of all that fear. Where there is fear there is no love, yes? Conversely where there is love, there is the absence of fear. So I set out to step through my fears so I could experience the love waiting on the other side. What are your fears? Where could you infuse them with the love they need to dissipate?

Fear, What is it Good For? Absolutely Nothing

If you're anything like me, you fear four main things—never solving your food issues, being fat, life itself, and people. Sound close? Most eating disordered people I have walked with concur this pretty much covers it. While that list encompasses most of life as we know it, did you know we are born with only two fears? Yup. Only two—falling and loud noises. Those make perfect sense to me—survival instincts basically. Our learned fears? They are ones you can choose to either feed or starve. For many years, you have likely fed them gourmet meals. You have ruminated about your lack of will power. You have obsessed about the "fact" that if you gave up bulimia, you will get fat. You fear you will never figure life out. You have hidden from anxiety producing people, places, and things. You have beaten yourself up for not being more this or that, for not connecting more deeply with people, for not living life more full out at times.

You will need to get connected with your soul to fully recover. This seems like such a mercurial concept. Lord knows you have likely tried many of the recommended things such as meditation, yoga, reading soulful books, healing retreats, and prayer, but the disconnect is ever-present, yes? Your mind and your soul are at war with one another. Your soul knows who you are—the light of the world, oneness with God, an extension of me yet uniquely you, love, purity, Divine wisdom—but your mind screams otherwise. It's time for integration.

Compassion Statements

Your internal dialogue is likely a mess, but how do you change it? You just do. This is the work. You dig deep, you think healthy thoughts, you record them, and you chew on them like you did your binge foods. You have compassion for yourself and for the many good things you do. You recognize yourself for who you are. You love your soul like it has never been loved. You spend time with kind and healthy thoughts until they become etched in your brain—until you are integrated with the truth.

Three compassion statement journal entries from my weaning stage are below. Please remember that I essentially loathed myself, so finding positive attributes felt wildly foreign. It might for you too, but I promise, there are thousands of things you could list. This is not a time for humility. It's time to have compassion. It's time to start seeing yourself as others around you do. It's time to notice all the wonderful things people say about you and start integrating them into your soul. This will ease the cognitive dissonance that so often drives your bulimia. Once you connect your thoughts with the ancient truth that your very soul emanates, change will be lasting.

February 7

- I am creating some awesome projects.
- People say I'm really warm and kind.
- I've had a very healthy day for my body.
- I always call friends and family members on their birthdays.
- I love my body and what it allows me to do.

February 11

- I am a productive self-starter.
- I am purpose driven.
- I am warm and friendly with others.
- I am honest and don't back stab.
- I am very creative.

February 14

- I am compassionate towards animals.
- I am a supportive wife.
- I am an adventurer who makes things happen.
- I don't wait for others to fulfill me.
- I am incredibly loyal to my friends and family.

Reading these compassion statements from many years ago, makes me both happy and sad. Happy because I was able to find things I loved about myself. Sad that at 44-years old these things were not already hardwired into my being. I often wonder what I could have accomplished thus far in life if I had a sense of confidence built into me from the beginning. My deep insecurity inevitably gave birth to anxiety. Anxiety then gave birth to various addictions. Various addictions gave birth to self-hatred. It was a self-fulfilling and self-perpetuating prophecy.

While we can never go back and change the past, we can adjust how we *think* about it. We can see things that seemingly happened *to* us as happening *for* us. We can choose to see the deep self-loathing and anxiety as the gateway to true love. Imagine if we never bubbled over into the realm of self-hatred (and I'm assuming since you are caught in a cycle of any addiction, there is an element of that), we would never have had to dig deep to transform that into self-love. If we just flat-lined an attitude like, *I'm not that bad,* or, *I don't really like myself that much, but I certainly don't hate myself,* then we might not have dug this deeply. We might not have found the inevitable full self-acceptance that comes with addiction recovery.

Once I started believing my compassion statements and getting soul connected, a wonderful thing began happening. My fears began to subside, and my outward connections became easier. Anxiety, once a ruling force, became just an annoying niggle. Once the raging war within began to subside, I could flow with life and with others. The only lasting way I know how to do that is by being soul connected to myself, my Source, and to others. If you feel disconnected, commit to writing out five compassion statements before you go to bed each night this week. Seeing the wonderful truth of who you are will help your mind and soul integrate.

Yoga to Heal Your Mind, Body & Soul

I already touched on how yoga is a wonderful addition to your recovery tool belt. But just to dive a little deeper into its benefits—yoga is medicine for integrating the body, mind, and soul. As I have, you have likely spent years hating or dissociating from your body. Your mind has tormented you, and your soul has felt empty. I think our souls feel sadness when witnessing the war raging between the mind and the body it's housed within. Our souls just want peace. They are peace. Your mind has tried for years to wrestle your body into submission, but nothing has worked. They are still at war with one another. And your soul is troubled. Mine was, too. But a few years ago, I stepped into a kundalini yoga class in Bali, and my soul did an immediate internal happy dance. I was home. The practice is phenomenal. While I have grown to love vinyasa, ashtanga, power, yin, nidra, and other more conventional forms of yoga, I think my soul will always feel most at home at kundalini. Instructors often ask the class if there are any newcomers that day. If someone raises their hand, they'll ask if the person has done any other forms of yoga. If she says yes, the leader will invariably say, "Great! It's nothing like that!"

Kundalini, called "the yoga of awareness" by practitioners, aims "to cultivate the creative spiritual potential of a human to uphold values, speak truth, and focus on the compassion and consciousness needed to serve and heal others." I would end that description with "heal ourselves and others" as that's what practitioners' experience. Kundalini is the term for "a spiritual energy or life force located at the base of the spine" and the practice of kundalini is designed to ignite this energy and transmit it through all the chakras to penetrate the crown chakra at the top of the head. Picture a spiritual chiropractic alignment. It also combines Bhakti yoga for devotion, Shakti yoga for power, and Raja yoga for mental power and control. It is also believed that kundalini yoga enables us to realize our Dharma or Life Purpose. I'll take some of that, please! And you?

Kundalini is not common in the west—you certainly won't find it on every street corner like many forms of yoga—so you will have to search out a studio and a seasoned yogi. And give it some time. I've had less than inspiring classes led by brand new instructors and mind-, soul-, and body-blowing classes led by 40+ year practitioners. So stick with it, and find a guru you love. And for those yogis who aren't yet seasoned, honor and bless them and trust you were in their class for a reason. Give everything you can to the practice, and see what magic happens. I've had experiences in a kundalini class akin to astral travel. No joke. It's a sure way to connect your mind, body, and soul with your Source. Which is a sure way to slow down and finally stop your need for bulimia.

One massive bonus I received during a class was that Truth dropped smack dab into my soul. Zam! It was palatable. For years after leaving the evangelical church that preaches Jesus is the *only* Truth, my prayer became, "Spirit, please show me Truth. Please burn away any indoctrination that is not Truth and make huge within me what is. Shrink one. Expand the other." That's really all I wanted. The Truth. During one of my first kundalini classes, the guru said to repeat the silent mantra Sat Nam—Sat on the inhale, Nam on the exhale. While I did that, peace penetrated my soul. I had never felt so present. She then said, "Sat Nam means Truth is my Identity." Bam! The Truth I'd searched for *out there* for decades was always within me. Inside of me. It *was* me.

I also practice what I've come to think of as regular yoga (those listed above) and it has been an invaluable coming home as well. My soul was longing for a spiritual connection, and I just couldn't find it anywhere else. I was raised in a non-religious or spiritual family, but after a long chain of events in my twenties, I eventually "surrendered to Jesus" and dove wholeheartedly into the Christian lifestyle. I taught Sunday school, led bible studies, spoke at women's conferences, committed to celibacy—the whole religious enchilada. But there were many things I could never reconcile. That's for another book. But, for now, I'll just say that the more steeped I became in the teachings of the Bible and modern-day Christianity, the less it made sense.

Leaving the church, while scary and humbling—I had been its advocate for so many years—also felt like the best gift I had ever given myself. While leaving rocked my foundation, my soul never felt freer. Please don't misunderstand me. I love that Christianity works for some and is there for those who connect with its teaching. And I love that Hinduism is there for those who connect with that. Buddhism resonates with so many others. True devoted Muslims love their God and people. I think God is Source, is Universe, is Oneness, is All-knowing, is All-loving, and humans would do really well to celebrate their faith and empower others to celebrate theirs. No right. No wrong. No division. This is what I found with yoga—oneness and love and mutual respect superseding any religious affiliation. I was home.

Obviously I'm a huge fan of yoga, but I mainly urge you to find some sort of mind, body, and soul integrative spiritual practice to call your own. Lean on it. Trust it. Use it for that chiropractic soul adjustment. If you do choose yoga, you will be loved in those rooms. Yogis are among the most inclusive, spiritual, loving, in-tune people I have met. Human and flawed, yes, but the very practice builds in a depth of character I haven't seen in any other people group. I understand yoga may not be for everyone, but my guess is it's for you, my dear sister. Try it. It just may reintroduce you to your soul.

What Would You Do if No One Was Looking?

Another aspect of feeding your soul is ensuring your vocation is in line with your values. If your work is not in alignment with who you are, your soul will starve. And a starving soul is the perfect escort for bulimia.

When I returned from rehab in 1995, I imagined I was expected to resume my career as Controller/Manager for a busy group of restaurants in Vancouver. It was fun and vibrant and exciting and lucrative, but was it supportive to my recovery? More importantly, would I be working there if no one was looking? In other words, did it make *me* happy, or did it quasi-fulfill some random expectation I either put on myself or a lifetime of messages put onto me? My gut told me not to return. But what was I to do?

I began asking myself, *what would I do if no one was looking?* This may seem totally obvious to you, but for me it was a revolutionary question. Where would I *love* to work? What career path would I *enjoy* pursuing? Would I start a business? Go back to school? What does my soul want— if I was the only person on the planet, what work would I do? It's an amazing question and one that I ask in many areas of life, not just career. If no one was looking would I still careen down the ski slope at Mach 3? Yes! If no one was looking would I still snuggle my dogs a ridiculous amount throughout the day? Yes! If no one was looking would I finish my pilot's license? No! The thought of my solo flight scared the crap out of me. It was not the good kind of fear that's fun to overcome—it was freaky kind of fear that warns you of impending death!

Again, I asked myself intently, *what would I do if no one was looking?* The answer? *Playing in gorgeous and colorful fabrics with happy and creative women making interesting and beautiful artwork and teaching others how to do the same.* As soon as I got the answer, I applied at a local quilt shop. What? Retail was so far below my "pay grade" but it was likely the most soul-caressing job I ever had. I didn't care if anyone was looking, and I had nothing to prove externally—this was simply how I wanted to spend my days.

I ended up doing the fabrics buying, teaching classes, and basically playing all day with women bathing in their creative juices. It was perfect. If your current job is not filling your soul, be courageous and make a change. It will be invaluable to your recovery process. The answers to this question will guide you right into the center of your true self.

Bulimia as a Band-Aid

For years I tried to rip off the Band-Aid of bulimia only to find a big gaping pus wound below, which would inevitably need another Band-Aid. It was a never-ending and painful cycle. I'm not sure how I never heard the following in two decades of searching, but when I finally did, it stuck. Addiction specialist, Dr. Gabor Maté, puts it so succinctly, "Addiction is simply pain avoidance." Ok, *that* I can get. The only caveat when it comes to bulimia is that a food addiction can also indicate being nutritionally starved. So not matter how much pain you eventually heal, you will still need to re-feed your body.

Taking into account the addiction-as-pain-avoidance model, it was totally futile to keep trying to rip off the Band-Aid (stop binging and purging) when that pain underneath was still acute. It became crystal clear that if I first healed the pain, the Band-Aid would become unnecessary, and the behaviors would subside. This seems a bit obvious to me now, but at the time it was revolutionary. So I got to work on the pain. Mine was different than yours, and yours will be different than the next person's, but it's there. Maybe your big sister didn't give you the time of day, or your brother purposely set you up for a fall, or your dad abandoned you, or your friends betrayed you. There will likely be many pain points along your life's journey. And if these aren't lovingly addressed and resolved, you'll likely need to keep using food to anesthetize yourself. Deep thought work will be necessary, but it needn't take years. Or even months. Pain can even be dealt with in an instant in some occasions. Simply changing your thoughts around each incident can be healing. Perhaps your sister was in deep despair herself, and your happiness illuminated her lack. Perhaps the only way your brother knew how to deal with his own demons was to fling them at you. Maybe your dad didn't leave you at all—it was the marriage he left. Maybe your friends were just in survival mode and needed to take down a perceived threat. The shift in these thought patterns makes it less about you and more about them and their pain. This doesn't change the incident, but it can dramatically change how you deal with each pain point. You can start to have compassion. You can respond rather than react. You can powerfully choose love.

This could be an entire book in itself, but in a nutshell, it will be really helpful for you to dig deeply and start to write down your pain points. Go to a quiet place with no distractions. Do whatever practice you do to get connected with your Source. Then ask to be shown the times in your life when you experienced acute pain. Allow whatever comes to come. It may come chronologically. It may come in degree of severity. It may be totally random. Write everything down, even if you don't understand it in the moment. Even if it doesn't really bring up pain. Trust your higher self. She knows what she is doing. She knows the pain points she wants to lead you to so they can be healed.

I hope some or all of these soul-healing suggestions will resonate with you. You are worth it. You are worth the work. You are worth healing. Your bulimia has been a beautiful beacon towards the path to self-love. Follow where it is taking you now. Follow it beyond itself and into recovery.

Freedom Exercises

1. Write five compassion statements before you go to bed every day for the next week. If this becomes a long-term daily habit, even better.

2. Ask yourself the tough question, "What would I do if no one was looking?" Include answers around not just your vocation, but who you spend time with, where you volunteer, what you read, what recreational activities you engage in, what you wear—anything that involves choice. Make sure they are yours, not ones society or old messaging has put on you.

3. Scan your life and list all the pain points that arise. Do what it takes to reconcile each one. It may be a conversation with a person involved, or it may be simply changing your thinking around the event.

4. List any other soul-strengthening activities you are committed to adding to your daily life.

CHAPTER 9

FREEDOM STRATEGY 7:
CREATING A LIFE YOU LOVE

"If we are facing in the right direction,
all we have to do is keep on walking."
—Zen Proverb

How are you doing so far? Are you feeling good about the idea of feeding your body so it's nutritionally full and feeding your soul so it's spiritually satisfied? I hope so—these two factors are necessary legs of the recovery stool. So is creating a life you love. Imagine waking up each day to 16-hours of time that you're not excited to fill? Then imagine a 16-hour period packed with goal-supporting and life-affirming activities? Creating a life you love will help you sustain solid recovery.

A Career to Serve Your Healing

We touched on this when considering the question, "What would you do if no one was looking?" But let's dig a little deeper here. Is your career serving your recovery, or is it fighting with it? I know two professional ballerinas who both came to the conclusion that they simply could not overcome their eating disorders while still in that business. They were faced daily with the need to be uber-thin which perpetuated the cycle. Similarly, a professional riding jockey friend said bulimia is rampant in the world of horse racing. For a race, he could only weigh a maximum of 119 pounds *including* his saddle, boots, and silks (uniform). Jockeys reduce their weight in a variety of ways, most being unhealthy. In fact, athletes in general are at a very high risk for developing an eating disorder. The National Athletics Trainers' Association estimates that as many as 62% of female and 33% of male athletes have disordered eating. Clearly an athletic career may not be conducive to your healing.

Ballerinas, jockeys, and other professional athletes are extreme cases—a certain physique or weight is required. But you don't need to be a pro athlete to be triggered by your vocation. Working in the restaurant business surrounded by food might be enough to trigger you. Or being a baker could seriously hinder recovery. Or the pressure of day trading might send you into a binge/purge episode in an attempt to ease the stress. Maybe the boredom and isolation experienced by truck drivers would be precarious. A triggering career could even be something seemingly benign—say, working in a care home that activates the pain you carry from having had an abusive grandparent. Only you will know if your job or career is supportive. If it is, stay. If not, it may be time for a change.

Fulfilling on Your Dreams & Goals

This may be a sobering question, but how many dreams and goals have you forfeited in the face of your bulimia? I know there are many. You are a deeply feeling, wildly creative, extremely capable woman. Women like you dream big.

As you enter into this serious and gritty stage of recovery, it will be helpful to revisit some of the many things you want to accomplish and experience in life. Start to dream again. Who would you be if you didn't struggle with bulimia? What activities could you do to support your recovery? Begin creating goal lists and strategies on how to accomplish them. This will become an important part of upgrading your life, free from bulimia. It may even be the key to your abstinence.

Keep in mind, a dream or goal doesn't have to be a big, huge tangible feat. It could simply be happiness. Happiness is, was, and will always be one of my life goals. What's life without happiness? But the question is, "How do I get happy?" My friend Anil Gupta, best selling author of *Immediate Happiness: Be Happy Now Using Practical Steps with Proven Results,* believes happiness can be realized through practicing the three Gs: Growth, Giving, and Gratitude. I would agree this is part of the equation. If we aren't growing, we are shrinking, which doesn't foster happiness. If we aren't giving, we are too self-absorbed to be truly happy. If we aren't grateful, how can we be happy? This all makes perfect sense.

In addition to the three Gs, I think there is a place for simply doing more of the stuff that really makes you smile. Bulimia can take you so far out of your own game of life that you forget how to even play. When was the last time you really belly laughed? Or were so focused on an activity that time stood still? Or were so dazzled by the beauty around you that your soul melted with the Universe? *These* are the types of activities I'm talking about. Some of my happy places are the dog park in West Vancouver, hitting the slopes at Whistler on a gorgeous spring day, snuggling my husband and pups on a Sunday morning in bed, riding the Sea to Sky highway on my motorbike, practicing vinyasa flow at Moksha Yoga in Phoenix, and hiking up to the dam with my mom in the Capilano Canyon. See how these are not Earth changing things? We don't have to get caught in the trap of thinking that dreams and goals have to be massive. Happiness can come, and I believe does come, in our seemingly incidental daily activities.

In fact, I think any goal you pursue is actually meant to create the *feelings* it will provide. For example, you may have a certain financial goal, but the feelings you are seeking from it could be freedom, significance, or power. Your goal may be to open a shelter for homeless dogs, but the feeling you are looking for is joy, connection, adventure, and love. You may have a goal to reach a certain weight, but what you are really looking for is to feel powerful, sexy, and happy. Conversely, you may have a goal to run a multi-million dollar business, but what you really want is to feel carefree. Just know that in the interim, this goal and desired feeling are not congruent. Similarly if you want to become an author, but you have a deep need to interact with and feel connected to others at this stage of your recovery, be aware that writing is an acutely solo endeavor. Your immediate goals and feeling needs may be fighting each other. For now, seek to have your feeling states as high as possible.

Take about 15-minutes, and write out all the feelings you want to feel and all the activities that bring about these feelings. Then commit to simply doing more of those things. If you are really stuck in a rut and even getting out to do the things you love seems hard, it will be helpful for you to reach out to others and set dates with them. They can be your happiness hounds. They will force you into doing the things you may not feel like in the moment, but things you know will do you wonders in the long run. It will serve you well. This new flow of positive energy will be the life force propelling you into abstinence. Energy breeds energy, so even if you don't *feel* like it in the moment, get out there and do the things you love. It will alter your state.

Doing the Next Right Thing

This leads to a really simple concept—do the next right thing. In early recovery and during life in general, feelings of overwhelm will arise. You'll be looking around your home or your office, and all you'll see is stress. It will show up as unfinished tasks, half read books, long to-do lists, goals you have yet to accomplish, or people you need to call. The urge to act out in your bulimia will become a force to contend with. Be prepared. The best advice I can give you is to simply do the next right thing. If you promised your friend or sponsor a phone call, then pick up the phone. If you told your neighbor you'd pick up the mail in her absence, go do that. If you committed to a yoga class that day, go grab your mat. Simply do that next right thing. When life becomes so overwhelming with tasks and possibilities, just get into action on one of those items. It will ease your stress immensely while guarding your abstinence.

To prepare for these times, it may be helpful to write a list of possible Next Right Things you can choose from. Sometimes in the moment, your brain will short-circuit and usher in your eating disorder. The more you can prepare for these moments, the more successful you will be able at navigating them. Try breaking up your list into short sections so the very list itself doesn't send you into overwhelm. Perhaps "At Home", "Outside Errands", and "Serving Others" can be a good way to start. If it's pouring rain or snowing, you may choose an "At Home" item like paying bills, cleaning out your lingerie drawer, bathing your dog, practicing your guitar skills, or researching a dream trip. On a sunny day, an "Outside Errand" like raking your yard, getting recovery supportive groceries, or washing your car might be more fun. When you really need to step outside yourself, perhaps choose something from the "Serving Others" list like visiting a rest home, walking an SPCA dog, volunteering at a homeless shelter, or helping your neighbor with her kids. You will know what to write on your lists. Just remember that simply doing the next right thing can make the difference between a day in recovery and a day in relapse.

Loving Your Home

One type of hunger, as explored earlier, is emotional hunger. This is one I still struggle with. If I'm not feeling emotionally well, my tendency is to hit the pantry. I know this is not the solution, but it was my default for so long, so it's a tough habit to crack. One emotion I try to nurture super lovingly is security—feeling physically safe and cocooned. Safety is a women's number one need, so it's one I suggest focusing on. One way I create a sense of safety is by making my home environment beautiful. Looking around at my nest with fondness reduces anxiety and diminishes my urge to eat the angst away.

When you look around your home, do you feel safe, secure, loved, cocooned? Is it supportive to your soul? Is it decorated in a style you love? Are things in good working order? Do you look around and see many things that make you smile? I hope so! You may wonder what this all has to do with binging and purging, but I promise you, the more peace you can create in your environment, the easier it will be to create peace in your mind, and the easier it will be to leave your bulimia behind.

This may seem a little woo-woo, but I went as far as hiring a Feng Shui consultant to give me ideas on how to bring even more chi (energy) into our home. A consistent flow of positive energy will no doubt bring positive results in your life. Shoot, even if it's the Placebo Effect, a beautifully Feng Shui-ed home can really help solidify your abstinence. You won't be constantly looking around at all the furniture you want to change, the electronics that need fixing, and the accessories you need to acquire to make your home complete. Instead, you will look around, be inspired, feel secure, and experience peace. It does not have to be expensive designer furniture and accessories either! You can do wonders with even the right second hand or discount store purchases.

Creating a home you love will usher in peace, help reduce your anxiety, and diminish the need to act out in your eating disorder. Even if to a small degree, it's worth it.

Stress Reduction

Another major factor in creating a life you love is stress management. Chronic stress taxes your endocrine system, wreaks havoc on your body and brain chemistry, and overloads your coping mechanisms. This is the perfect storm for emotional eating and exaggerated cravings for comfort and energy. Human studies have shown an increased preference for high sugar foods in those reporting greater stress exposure. Daily stressors are also associated with unhealthy snacking. Keep life as Zen as possible, especially during early recovery.

Stress can be insidious and comes in many forms. It can include health challenges, interpersonal relationship issues, financial limitations, death of a loved one, relocating, national economic or political unrest, personal trauma, job pressure, environmental toxins, loud noises, overwhelming responsibilities, and any significant loss. Stress can also show up internally via the thoughts and expectations you put upon yourself.

There are many different stress reduction techniques and strategies. The main thing is to find some that work for you, and do them consistently. When you feel the need to soothe your stress with food, instead try one of the following activities:

- Take a walk in nature.
- Cuddle your pet.
- Call a friend.
- Listen to inspiring audio books or podcasts.

- Take a warm bath or shower.
- Breathe deeply for five minutes.
- Journal about your feelings.
- Play your favorite instrument.
- Mediate, pray, chant.
- Paint, sew, knit.
- Take a yoga class.
- Do some gardening.
- Did I say, breathe?

Recovery Dog

If you're not a dog lover, switch this to a recovery cat, turtle, guinea pig, whatever! If possible, just make sure you have something alive that brings you joy and that you need to care for. If you already have kids, you likely have your hands full, but if you are the only living thing in your household, getting something to take care of outside yourself could be helpful. I got my sweet Whippet puppy, Parker, when I was still in full-blown bulimia. I was also single and had been living on my own for years. The silence and stillness at home were killing me. Parker became my little angel. She came everywhere with me—to the office, to my real estate projects, to friend's houses, on walks, on hikes, even on trips. I'm not sure what would have become of me without that beautiful soul. Sometimes I wonder if I would even be here.

Is there a furry or scaly or feathered creature that might bring joy to your life? Could it become symbolic of your commitment to recovery?

Channel Your Creativity

Have you ever noticed the high incidents of drug and other addictions in the creative world—musicians, artists, writers, dancers, and actors? It seems to me that it's a remarkable percentage. It makes me wonder if creative types are simply more prone to addiction. Perhaps the genius that makes some humans so creative and willing to explore is the flip side of the coin of substance abuse. Sometimes the incredibly intense creative juices, if not channeled, just *have* to be squelched.

Have you ever just jammed on a creative project, and then something derails you, and the juice gets stuck? It becomes such an intense stuck-ness that you go and use food to calm the anxiety instead of pushing through and getting the juice flowing again? I wonder if musicians who overdosed, did so when they were thwarting their creativity. It can seem that way for me. For example, even during writing this book, there have been times when I have jammed out 3,000 words in a sitting. Other times, 300. Guess what my robot mind wants to do when I'm stuck? You've got it—hit the fridge. But when I resist the urge and just hunker down and create, the urge subsides. It takes mental discipline, but it's doable.

One recovering bulimic I mentored is an absolutely incredible painter. Her love of animals and acrylics combine to create the most beautiful canvases. It was always clear to me when she was struggling with relapse as photographs of any new artwork stopped pinging into my in-box. I suspected bulimia was luring her away from the easel, and all those visions within her were left unexpressed. But now she is bulimia-free, and her creations are flowing endlessly again. The world is a more beautiful place when she is walking in recovery. The same is true for you.

Do you have creative projects bubbling up within you that have been put on hold by bulimia? Lovingly ask yourself, *how do I feel at 90 years old, looking back on life having not completed those creative projects?* Note this. Feel it. Live from that place of regret, even if just for a moment. Ask yourself if your bulimia was worth it. Then fast forward to 90 years old again and ask, *how do I feel having fulfilled my creative dreams?* Notice the emotion you feel. Look at the sparkle in your 90-year-old eyes. Notice the surroundings. Are your paintings hung on the wall? Are the quilts you sewed donning the beds? Is your garden blooming with flowers and flourishing with veggies you planted and nurtured? Your creativity could be the link to your recovery. Don't ignore those urges—channel them.

Connection with Others

One thing common among bulimics is isolation. Regarding food, you have likely done what you want, when you wanted, and have done it alone. This was your habitual cycle. But recovery can't look that way. You will have to come out of hiding. Don't worry, you won't have to jump out all at once, but you will need to make small steps towards integrating with healthy people and activities.

You've already done this in Freedom Strategy 1 to a certain degree, but there's a difference between peeking your head out the window and doing a swan dive into the pool below. While it may take some time and some practice dives, it's the latter I'm hoping you'll become an expert in. I'm still not fully there. It can be a life-long process. Especially if you are more introverted by nature, and my guess is you are. You're also likely an HSP (Highly Sensitive Person), a term coined by Dr. Elaine Aron. According to her research, this trait is common among 15-20% of the population and effectively means that your survival instinct is super strong and that your brain works a little differently than the less sensitive 80-85% of people. It is an innate trait and manifests as a greater awareness of your surroundings and causes you to be more easily overwhelmed. I definitely identify as being an HSP, so swan diving into social settings is a little harder for me. Living there, even more so. But isolation is fodder for bulimia. We need to consciously connect with others to stay in recovery. You may want to go back to your things-I-love-to-do list, choose activities that do involve people but don't revolve around food, and commit to exploring them one-by-one. Perhaps join a drop-in badminton league or a hiking club or a book study. Anything that will support your recovery and help you connect with people.

Plan a Trip

Part of creating a life you love is having adventures that take you out of your reality. They are called vacations for a reason—you *vacate* your normal daily existence. I highly recommend you spend some time thinking about a soul-enriching and recovery-supporting trip. Not one that may harm you. If your weakness is popcorn and candied apples, for example, I wouldn't suggest Disneyland. My happy place is high-altitude trekking. It fully supports my recovery. My love of connecting with people over a physical activity is met, my love of experiencing foreign cultures is met, my love of pushing myself physically is met, my love of fresh air and nature is met, and my love of adventures is met. It also meets my need for autonomy, as I always trek with girlfriends rather than as a couple with my husband. The more you meet your needs legitimately, the less you will try to meet them through your bulimia.

Your focus going forward is to create a life you love—including an empowering career, a cozy home, companions to share with, creative hobbies, and doing more of the things you love. This will help you access lasting recovery. No matter what your actual bulimic behaviors are at this point, make it your focus to begin creating the life your soul wants to lead. It will bring you a level of happiness that is incongruent with your bulimia, and bulimia will begin to lose its grip.

Freedom Exercises

1. Ask yourself if your career is helping or hindering your recovery. Then make changes accordingly.
2. List a dozen activities that bring you happiness, and commit to exploring each of them over the coming months.
3. Make a list of "Next Right Things" you can do when faced with the urge to binge/purge.

4. Commit to creating a home environment that serves your recovery.

5. Make a list of ten stress reducing activities you can draw from when needed.

6. Begin exploring a creative hobby. It can be something dormant you've done in the past or something new you think you'll love.

7. Write the name of a few people or groups you'd like to connect with more deeply, and then commit to reaching out.

CHAPTER 10

FREEDOM STRATEGY 8: MAKING PEACE WITH FOOD & YOUR BODY

*"You can't separate peace from freedom because
no one can be at peace unless he has his freedom."*
—Malcolm X

While Malcolm X was not speaking about peace and freedom around food, this quote totally applies to your struggle. For years you have been at war with food and your body, yes? *Should I eat this? Oooh, that's way too much. Wow, I can't possibly even start on that. Man my body feels lumpy. If I could only lose just a few more pounds. My clothes are so damn tight.* Sound familiar? Not very peaceful, right?

Imagine if those battles each came to an end, and freedom ensued. Imagine if you could replace the mounting and constant pressure to be a certain shape and to eat the right foods in the appropriate quantities with an abiding peace and love of food and your body? Food is supposed to nourish you and bring you joy. Your body is meant to serve you and enable you to live your best life. Somehow those things got totally derailed when bulimia came on board. But you can get back on track. Let's explore some ideas on how to reconcile with food and your body.

The Food War is Futile

Given your years of battling food with no lasting results, can you make a personal declaration? Can you simply state that what you are doing is not working? Imagine if two countries warred for decades with no peaceful resolution in sight? All that remains would be a swath of death and destruction. It's the same with bulimia. It's a never-ending battle until you decide the war is over, but you alone have the power to lay down the metaphorical sword. It will take effort. It will take support. It will take a massive amount of self-love and chutzpah, but believe in yourself. You can do this.

Making Peace with Food

Other than making peace with your body, making peace with food may be the hardest part of recovery. It's imperative and could take years to master. I don't say that to discourage you. I say it so you have compassion for yourself. I have to confess, a few extra pounds have made their way to my waistline as I wrote this book—Paleo crackers with almond butter have an amazing way of breaking through writer's block, loneliness, and boredom. Never really successfully, but I have many moments of unwillingness I still need to manage. Making peace with food might have to be my daily practice for years to come, and I accept that. I'm so proud of myself to even be able to eat crackers and almond butter alone in my house without it turning into a binge. So I focus on that and give myself grace. You can too. Be patient.

One strategy we've touched on before is to become aware of your hunger and try to eat only when your body is actually asking for food. If your supposed hunger is really thirst, drink water instead. If your hunger is highlighting an emotional need, get that need met in a more effective way than food will offer. If your hunger is really a need for connection for example, call a friend. Or are you trying to avoid feeling pain? Perhaps journaling will help more than Jujubes. If you can't figure out what it really is—you just want food and you want it now—it could also be a simple nutritional need. Have you been feeding yourself supportive foods? Maybe you need to amp up your intake of healthy greens. Once your body is nutrient rich, your survival instincts will no longer scream for high calorie and sugary foods. Do this for yourself lovingly. Even as you chop veggies, thank yourself for giving this amazing gift to your body. Be sure to eat high quality proteins such as 100% grass-finished beef, wild caught fish, and cage-free eggs. Healthy fats are imperative also. Avocados, coconut oil, flax seed oil, olive oil, certain nuts, and almond butter will serve your body and your mind well. Remember, you may need to rely heavily on your support systems to counter the barrage of negative thoughts as you begin to make peace with food.

Another strategy we've touched on is journaling. Journaling takes the mess of thoughts swirling around your head causing stress and dumps them onto paper where they can be seen for what they are. Sometimes the thoughts are so irrational that all you can do is laugh seeing them in black and white. Other times, they are very true and seeing them on paper can be the necessary catalyst for change—writing can help you face the music. Journaling also helps you get clarity around decisions. It's astounding. When you start writing, your own inner voice gets activated and decisions you once thought confusing and impossible, become clear and easy to make.

Journaling is also helpful to record your food choices throughout the day. There are numerous studies indicating you will have more success in creating healthy food patterns in the future if you record your patterns today. It can be easy and fun. In early recovery, I recorded my entire daily intake in an iCal event on my iPhone called *Food Love*. The name was to remind myself that's what food is supposed to be—love for our bodies. I had such a love/hate relationship with food for so long that I needed a daily reminder to only focus on the love. In the notes, I simply record what I'd eaten that day. I began to see food as a way to love my body. The words *Food Love* also helped me create gratitude and peace around nourishment. I jotted down little notes about how I felt emotionally and any insights that came up around my choices as well. It was a great tool and one I highly suggest for you to implement if you sense it will support your recovery.

This part of the journey can be tough. There is no magic pill for making peace with food. Success will come only from flexing healthy food muscles. Slowly and deliberately. The more you flex, the easier it will become. I'm not going to sugarcoat anything. I sit here almost four years abstinent, and the battle still swirls around me. But it has changed—what was once a raging nuclear war with no hope of victory is now one where victory has been won. The enemy still tries to storm the castle from time to time, so vigilance is key. Maybe some people recover and gain instant freedom, and that's amazing! My story has been more turtle-like. That's all I know, so it's the perspective from which I share.

How can you begin to make peace with food? Do you have any strategies to add? I know food has seemed like your enemy also, but see if you can start to shift your thinking around it. That coupled with implementing some practical strategies will help peace flourish.

The Hunger Scale

During early recovery, eating to feed my body's needs, not my taste bud's cravings, never even occurred to me. I really didn't care what my body needed and sure didn't know how much it needed. Managing the physical sensations of hunger and satiety was a learned skill. For so many years, I either loved the starving feeling or ate to the point of explosion. I missed the whole middle ground. In fact, moderate satiety felt incredibly uncomfortable and brought up fear. But it's where we need to live three to five times per day, so we should embrace it now rather than fight it forever.

The hunger/fullness scale goes something like this:

1. Severe hunger. You feel like you could eat anything in sight. You are perhaps weak or lightheaded. You are very much at risk for a binge.
2. Stomach growling hunger. You feel a strong physical need for food. You may feel irritated. You are at risk for a binge.
3. You feel like eating, but you have no physical symptoms. This is the best time to eat as your risk for binging is diminished.
4. Mild hunger. You feel like nibbling on something small to satiate your body's very slight sensations.
5. You have eaten and you are no longer hungry. You sense an appropriate amount of food in your system. You are satisfied. This is the best time to stop eating.
6. You are no longer hungry, but the food is so tasty that you keep eating. Your mind says you no longer need food, but your taste buds want more. If you keep eating, you are at risk for a binge.
7. You have overeaten and are uncomfortable. You beat yourself up emotionally. You feel like you've blown it and tell yourself you might as well eat more.
8. If you do, you are now beyond full. You are stuffed and feel deep regret for your actions. You have lost your peace with food, and your body and mind are paying the price. It will be hard for you to overcome the urge to purge.

Ideally, you should oscillate between a three and a five throughout the day. This would keep your mind and your body very happy. Of course this will not always be the case! You might wake up ravenous or you may get stuck in a meeting that pushed mealtime back by a few hours. Life happens. You will likely overeat from time to time, whether by choice or by habit. The main thing is to notice these and manage them effectively. When you need to call for support, do so right away.

Eating & Food Tactics

This brings us to a few thoughts about *how* you are eating and managing food. Do you eat slowly and with gratitude? Do you mainly eat alone? Are trigger foods continually in your space? Are you afraid to waste food?

One of the defining characteristics of a binge is the wildly rapid pace of ingestion. To counter that habit, make a concerted effort to slow down. Chew your food. Savor the flavor. Also, notice it. Turn the TV off. Close the book. Put the magazine aside. Actually look at and acknowledge your food. Thank it. The slower and more mindfully you eat, the healthier your food attitude will become. Also, be mindful of all that went into its production. Mentally thank the family or company that farmed it. Thank the truckers who transported it. Thank the shop owners who risked their finances and time bringing you this gift of food. The more connected you can get, the more grateful you become, and the less likely you will abuse it. Make it a practice of giving thanks each time you sit to a meal. Appreciation ushers in peace.

Another strategy to help you make peace with food is to call in the troops! I asked myself, "Should I eat or not eat?" hundreds of times as I was trying to get well. I was overly hungry, but I was alone. A disastrous combo. If this is your story, during this laying-down-the-sword part of the process, you may need others to help keep you abstinent. Safe meal dates can be just the answer. Ask your support person for her help and accountability. This is totally opposite to your normal tendency of isolation and eating alone, but that never worked, right? Time for a new strategy.

You will also be wise to avoid your trigger or cascading foods—those you know that having just one will cascade into a full-blown binge. Remember the potato chip ads citing, "I bet you can't have just one?" They were smart advertisers. Avoiding trigger foods entirely may seem very black and white and pretty hard-core, but in my experience over 20+ years of trying and failing and trying again and working with others with the same experience, I believe there are certain foods I simply can't have, ever. They are not supportive to my body, my mind, or my recovery. The data on sugar addiction is especially interesting. If I let myself go there and just "cheat" once, I inevitably fight this squirrely mind for days as my body screams for more.

If certain foods have this effect on you, you may even be allergic to them. During a reaction called allergic addiction, your body releases powerful chemicals that soothe your brain in an attempt to soothe the physical allergic reaction. These soothing neurochemicals can become addictive, giving birth to a self-fulfilling allergic/addictive cycle. Food allergies not only set you up for a binge, they also adversely affect your emotions, memory, body temperature regulation, sexual appetite and function, blood pressure, sleep patterns, hunger, and thirst. So if you can strategize to avoid just that first bite, you won't be thrown into the addictive and damaging cycle. Begin to identify as someone who simply doesn't eat that food. This is a bit controversial as many will say that restricting something will keep you in the eating disordered cycle—the old *everything in moderation* meme comes to mind. But everything in moderation can lead to health in moderation. So for now, I'm just suggesting you do your best to avoid those foods you know don't support you and may set you up for a fall. You can play around with them later in your recovery as you put more and more time between yourself and your last episode.

Make it easy on yourself at home in this stage of recovery—as mentioned in the Detox Your Kitchen section—purge your pantry of all trigger and cascading foods as well as those you suspect you are allergic to. Someone deeply struggling with bulimia had me into her home recently. When she opened the pantry cupboard to get some bottled water, I was shocked by what I saw. Shelves upon shelves of processed and unsupportive foods, chocolates, muffins, crackers, and candy. As you begin the process of making peace with food, it's best to avoid having to stare down binge foods each time you open a cupboard. Studies indicate that willpower is a finite resource. You'll eventually cave.

Shopping daily will also help reduce your temptation to binge and therefore your likelihood of purging. I learned this strategy while nannying in France when I was 18 and pulled it out years later as I was trying to recover. While the North American shopping model looks more like a weekly stock up of packaged foods full of chemical preservatives or even produce that somehow manages to stay fresh all week, Europeans tend to bring home truly fresh food daily from the butcher, fish monger, deli, dairy, and farmer's market. It's a beautiful practice. If you live alone, bring home only what you will need for that day or evening. If you have a family, bring home just enough to feed everyone. Leftovers were highly triggering for me in early recovery and are still a bit of a hurdle. Maybe it's the same for you? If so, daily shopping can become a beautiful and mindful recovery ritual.

Delighting in wastage will also be helpful in your quest to make peace with food. This may seem strange, but it will reduce the amount of control food has over you. Food is meant to serve *you*, not the other way around. I grew up in a family where, "Waste not, want not," was spoken often. In other words, if you waste anything, you better not ask for anything more. It was spoken tongue-in-cheek, but it was also our reality—we really didn't waste much of anything. If the bread was getting a bit dry and hard, breakfast became French toast. If the bananas went rotten, it was time to make banana bread. Turkey carcass? Homemade soup of course! All these examples are totally responsible and good practices. Nothing negative about them at all. We learned the value of things, and I appreciate that. My grandparents lived through the depression, so it's no wonder my parents learned it was a waste to throw anything away. Food was basically never discarded. Plates were always eaten clean, and leftovers were golden.

I carried that view for most of my life until I heard my Auntie Bev say, "Better to go to waste than to your waist!" I loved this. Yes, it's true, if you're overeating just to clean the plate, you're wasting it anyhow, so you might as well just give it to the garbage. Another common thing we've all heard is, "Eat it. There are kids starving in Africa!" True, there are. But you eating or not eating that last bite on your plate that your stomach has no room for won't help them in the slightest.

The last food tactic you may find helpful is practicing some sort of gratitude ritual before eating. Whether you are religious, agnostic, or an atheist, you can do this. The Judeo-Christian model is to bow your head, give thanks for the meal, and ask it to be used to nourish and bless your body. The Hindu heritage believes food is the physical manifestation of the supreme universal energy and Hindus pray that those providing the food experience an abundance of health and happiness. Muslims praise Allah before eating as the one who gave them the food and called them to be Muslims. Buddhist's also have a specific pre-meal gratitude prayer, as do Jewish people, Native Americans, and other groups throughout the world. It will be helpful for you to adopt one of these prayers or come up with your own pre-meal ritual to ground you and bring about mindfulness. It can be as simple as thanking every hand that went into its production or thanking your body for using it to help you live a wonderful life. Come up with something that resonates for you, then practice that ritual before each meal.

Strategies for Socializing

Social functions revolving around food used to traumatize me—especially buffets. While I love people and wanted to connect, tables of food were barriers. If I was at one end of the room enjoying an interaction, the buffet at the other end would be screaming out at me, "Get OVER here!" But I knew I could not. I couldn't even risk one small plate. If I could just get through the bulk of the evening without eating, I would not risk a binge and have to bolt. If I didn't quite have the willpower and caved, I would end up in a funky place of giving a quarter of my attention to the people around me and the rest of my attention to the piles of food. It's no wonder I avoided many social environments. Fighting food was torturous. But as I committed to starving the binge beasts instead of starving myself, they no longer controlled me. Their voices screamed less often and less loudly I now love social settings, even if food is the centerpiece.

Here are a few tips to help you enjoy functions involving food as well:

- Before leaving home, have some water and a few nuts or sliced veggies so you don't get to the dinner or party ravenous.
- Avoid the appetizer buffet and pass on the canapés. This can lead to mindless munching.
- At a sit down dinner, either forgo an appetizer or choose a nutritionally supportive green salad. A main course alone is usually more than enough food to bring you to a level five satiety.
- Stick to one helping. Seconds usual fall into emotional eating. Connect more deeply with your dining companions instead.
- If you really must have dessert, JJ Virgin, best-selling author of *The Sugar Impact Diet* suggests sticking to the three-bite rule. Your sweet tooth or craving will have long since been satisfied

during those three bites. Anything after that just becomes unnecessary overindulgence.

- Avoid excess alcohol. It is completely void of nutrients and will diminish your resolve to maintain healthy eating habits.

Above and beyond these strategies, be sure to practice mindfulness and gratitude. Be present to your thoughts and feelings. Be grateful for the humans you have been invited to interact with. Try your best to stay in the moment. Be present. You are a social creature, but bulimia has you slightly out of practice. Isolation has rusted your party skills to a degree. But they are a cinch to polish and can be restored easily to their pre-eating disorder glory. Just keep mindfully trying!

Loving Your Body

This has perhaps been my biggest challenge. I just couldn't imagine fully loving my body unless I was a stick figure. Body Dysmorphic Disorder (BDD) ruled my mind and my mirrors for as long as I can remember. Wiggling out of its grip has been almost as impossible as wiggling out of my skinny jeans. I even bought myself an expensive pair of 34Bs in my 30s thinking that would help. All the teasing I got in my teens and twenties for having mosquito-bites (that was generous) had taken its toll. But even that didn't help.

In counseling, Cesar said that loving your body will likely be the last piece of the eating disorder recovery puzzle to find its place. He said clinical research indicates that it takes about one year of normalized eating before the body stabilizes and body love starts to kick in. This was certainly true for me. Actually, I'm still waiting for it to fully kick in. After being objectified for so many years, it's pretty hard to really understand that you are more than just your body, your appearance, or your athleticism. Old thoughts die hard. But I did find certain things helpful in the transformation from body loather to body lover.

One thing for sure—throw away the scale! Yes, do it. You are not a number. Your day should not be a success or a failure based on digits staring up at you from a one-foot by one-foot hunk of plastic and electronics. Your happiness should not depend on whether the numbers were lower or higher than the day before. The only exception is if you have such bad BDD that the number on the scale *helps* you see you are not as large as your mind is telling you. If it will support your recovery, keep the scale, and limit using it to once per week.

Similarly, discard disempowering mirrors. You know the ones! There are some that are totally warped, and no matter how loose your clothes are fitting these days, the mutant mirror shows you as being massive. This is not helpful. Better yet, get yourself a skinny mirror. We've all seen those, too! In early recovery, I had gained a few pounds and was really struggling with embracing my healthier body. My husband and I were on a trip, and I looked in the hotel mirror and thought, *you look hot!* These were not words that came to my mind very often, so I was certain it was the mirror. Sure enough, Ken said he looked slimmer in it also. Caveat: slim is *not* the goal. Creating healthy eating habits and cultivating an empowering body image are. I'm just saying that in the early stages, do *everything* you can to feel beautiful and empowered. If a trick mirror helps, I'm all for it. During that trip I was so much happier without the constant barrage of negative body thoughts coursing through my mind.

Another way to feel better in your own skin is to create an empowering wardrobe. Please chuck those teeny tiny jeans you haven't fit into very well since you were a bit on the skeletal side. You were unhealthy and only an unhealthy body (and mind) will fit those again. Add pieces that cause you to think, *Damn, I look great!* You should be able to go to your closet on any occasion and find something you feel empowered wearing. Ditch items you don't enjoy, and add some you do. Make a game of this—for each week you don't binge and purge, you get to buy a new piece of clothing. This is totally doable! Think of all the money that used to go down the toilet.

As you begin to have small measures of success in your recovery, cultivating gratitude for your body will become easily. But in the meantime, you may have to proactively bring gratitude to the top of your mind. This will be super worthwhile as the more gratitude you cultivate, the less emotional hunger will assault you. The more you love your body, the less you will want to abuse it. Make a list of all the things your body enables you to do. Are you a hiker? Skier? Runner? Consider everything you do that's physical, and then thank your body for allowing you to do each thing. What you look like won't give you long-term happiness. What you do won't either, but athletic accomplishments are a lot more interesting than just looking pretty. Begin practicing gratitude for what your body *does* rather than how it looks. It is a vehicle to your dreams, not an ornament.

As you imagine all the movement-oriented things your body allows you to do, ask yourself, *Do I feel great in what I'm wearing when I do them?* It may seem as frivolous as making sure you love your wardrobe, but having a few exercise outfits you enjoy will make you more likely to move regularly. Get yourself some sassy gear. It's not 100% necessary, but it can be surprisingly supportive. I suggested this to one gal who then shocked herself by how much more she hit the hiking trail in her new duds. Treat yourself and watch the body love follow. And now that you have the empowering gear, get out and move. Do you like to hike? Practice yoga? Play tennis? If you're not active now, think back to your childhood—what did you like to do then? Whatever it was, take Nike's advice—just do it. Movement will help you integrate with your body, and integration is the precursor to love.

Lastly, the most important, and likely the hardest part of loving your body, is to embrace the one you have today. It's the only one you've got or will ever have. Tomorrow's body will never come. The one you embody now has been with you since your first breath and will be with you until your last. Every day it is doing so much for you—it is carrying you from adventure to adventure, from friendship to friendship, from disease to health, from home to work and back, and from activity to activity. I remember being in the Body Image class in rehab, and the question was posed, "What is your perfect body." There were many answers from athletic, to boyish, to hour-glass, to willowy. But, for me the perfect body is the poolside woman, completely unaware of the few rolls around her waist, the bit of cellulite on her bum, or the wiggle in her arms. She is so busy having fun that all you notice is joy emanating from her. *That* is the perfect body. That is *my* goal, and that is my hope for you.

While some of the previous strategies seem contrary to this final wish, it's because they are. Ideally, if I looked into a mirror, I would love what I saw no matter if it was a "skinny" or a "fat" mirror. Ideally, I wouldn't care if I had a sassy exercise outfit or a bulky grey sweat suit. The bottom line is that my eating disordered and body dysmorphic disordered mind isn't quite there yet. Is this true for you? If so, do your best to hack it. The time will come when you love your body unconditionally, but in the meantime, do what you can to at least like it.

My friend and mentor, Taryn Brumfitt, author of *Embrace: My Story from Body Loather to Body Lover* and founder of the global phenomenon *The Body Image Movement*, says, "We live in a beauty-obsessed society, and we've been preyed upon and reprogrammed by the diet and beauty industry to want to be something other than what we are." I fully agree with her.

So let's stand up, take back our power, and embrace the bodies we have. Let's love them so thoroughly that we can't even imagine abusing them like we once did. This might seem impossible in early recovery. Can you imagine actually accepting and loving your body? It might be a totally foreign concept after all the years of manipulating it through exercise, starvation, surgery, and whatever else promised that perfect figure. Can you finally give up the fight? Can you simply surrender and embrace it? All of it? As it is?

Freedom Exercises

1. Start a food journal if this feels helpful to you.
2. Purge your closet of any disempowering clothing. Your local Goodwill or secondhand store will be delighted.
3. Purchase one pair of jeans you feel absolutely fabulous wearing.
4. Get a sassy exercise outfit or two.
5. Look in the mirror everyday for the next week, and tell yourself how amazing your body is. Tell yourself you are sexy. You are strong. You are awesome. For this exercise, the old adage of *fake it till you make it* may come in handy. It did and still does for me.
6. Now write down at least 20 body parts you love. These can be visual traits or activities each part allows you to do. For example, *I love my beautiful fingernails* or *I love how my strong thighs allow me to ski like a maniac.* Hopefully there will be a healthy blend of both. Gratitude will be a major key to you embracing your body. The more you can think these thoughts, the less you will obsess about what you don't like. Review this list as often as you need for it to sink into your soul.

CHAPTER 11

FREEDOM STRATEGY 9: CULTIVATING GRATITUDE

"Gratitude makes sense of our past, brings peace for today, and creates a vision for tomorrow."
—**Melody Beattie**, *Choices: Taking Control of Your Life and Making It Matter*

I remember exactly where I was when my orthopedic surgeon called with my test results. And I can almost taste the tear that dripped down my cheek when he told me the news. "Simply repairing the labrum will do you no good. It tore because you have hip dysplasia. You will need a full hip replacement."

Okay, that pretty much sent me into a meltdown. Who at 42 years old needs a hip replacement? It was a devastating blow. At the time, I was an avid runner, and if I didn't do some sort of resistance training daily as well, my mind went nutty. How was I going to maintain sanity while being sedentary after major surgery?

My first question back to the surgeon was, "Will I ever run again?" I didn't like the answer.

This could have been the single worst bit of news I had ever received. That shows you how fortunate I've been. But for an exercise addict with bulimia and body dysmorphic disorder, it was pretty much devastating. At least it would have been if I hadn't already been practicing gratitude. It was time to step up. It's one thing to say you have a beautifully deep gratitude practice, but how is it when faced with a seemingly terrible situation. This is the true test.

After the initial shock and grief wore off, I went to work reigning in my thoughts, as they were wildly depressing and dramatic. I'll spare you the details, but suffice to say they were dark and hopeless. To pull myself out of the despair, I went about changing my thinking. How we view our challenges is the key to living a happy and grateful life. Rather than spiraling, I replaced the negative thoughts with more positive ones like:

- I'm so lucky I live in a nation where this level of medical care is available.
- I'll eventually be out of pain.
- I'll officially be a Bionic Woman!
- I'll get to challenge myself further—rather than just accomplishing my next trek to Everest Base Camp for example, I'll get to do it with a titanium hip! Pretty novel.
- I'll get lots of TLC from my husband.

Do you see how gratitude helped change the entire scenario? You may wonder what this has to do with recovering from bulimia, but I can tell you without a doubt that the shift in mental energy gratitude brings will shift your ability to quit bulimia and upgrade your life. This part is all in your thinking. And cultivating a grateful mindset will serve you well.

Before, during, and after my hip replacement, my thinking was remarkably positive. Hell, I was so amazed with my mindset Eckhart Tolle would have been impressed. Then, two months into my healing, I jumped on my motorbike for the first time and almost got hit by an elderly man in an SUV who "just didn't see me." He cut right in front of me into a neighboring driveway. I have been riding for 15 years, have ridden hundreds of thousands of miles, and have never had an accident. But here I was, *just* recovering from one major surgery and wham! To avoid being killed, I pirouetted off my bike, threw it at the broadside of the truck, and landed on the pavement. It was a close call. But I was unscathed—or so I thought.

As with the orthopedic surgeon's words about my hip dysplasia, I'll always remember the emergency doctor at St. Luke's saying, "You've completely shattered your elbow and will need extensive reconstructive surgery." Geez. Really? After the tears flowed—from a combination of pain, exhaustion, shock, and disbelief—it was time to put on my big girl gratitude panties again. This was not going to take me down the rabbit hole of regret and pity. Instead, I thought things such as:

- I could have been killed and wasn't.
- This is a lesson to always wear protective riding gear in the future.
- The whole thing was caught on camera, so there was no disputing whose fault it was.
- I have insurance.
- I'll get lots of TLC from my husband. (This was a reoccurring theme.)

Can you see how I could have chosen to be a victim in both cases, but refrained? Being a victim would have served my eating disorder, but not my recovery. What situations are you facing in your life that you are tempted to complain about? Think of three seemingly tough ones, and write them down. Where can you alter your thinking to be more powerful and supportive of your recovery? Ponder these new thoughts instead. You can literally rewire your thinking and reframe each circumstance. I'm not saying to bury your true emotions. For sure I cried over facing hip and elbow surgeries back to back like that, but then once I had felt the feelings, I let them go. I released them and moved to the next stages—acceptance and then gratitude.

I believe gratitude is the foundation for your healing. You can take any of your life's negative experiences and turn them into positive ones. Make a game of it, and see the new, fresh, clean energy flowing to you and through you. This will help diminish the negativity that has accompanied your bulimia.

There is a reason for your struggle. Your bulimia has created in you a strength you would never had cultivated without it. Think of the butterfly wrestling to escape its cocoon. The struggle causes beauty and strength. It's the same with you. You are a strong, courageous, beautiful creature with so much to be thankful for. Make it a habit to cultivate gratitude in every situation. Think of the glorious planet you live on, the intense sun that provides light and warmth, the clean water you have on-demand, and your bodily systems that miraculously keep you alive without your conscious effort. Think of your friends, your family, your pets, your health, your passions, and your hobbies. You have a wonderful life in so many ways!

Bulimia can seem all-consuming and can feel like it blackens your entire existence, but don't forget to be grateful for the other 99% of your life. Make gratitude a daily practice. I have a reoccurring daily iCal event

I simply call *Gratitude*. It prompts me each night to think of three things I'm grateful for that occurred during the day. Going to sleep with these things top of mind is a sweet way to drift off.

Thank Your Bulimia

Here is where things get real. If you can come to a place where you can actually *thank* your bulimia, it will be easier to release it. Yes, practice gratitude for the very thing you likely hate about yourself the most. Once you shift your attitude, your shame will be replaced with self-respect, your secrets will give way to sincerity, and bondage will be exchanged for freedom. You will begin to live in the light rather than in darkness. Let's dig to see where you can change your attitude towards your eating disorder. A good place to start is by writing a list of all the things bulimia has provided for you. It may seem hard at first, but trust that it will begin to flow. Here are a few ideas to get you going:

- Bulimia relieved your stress and anxiety.
- It was your friend when you were lonely.
- It kept you from feeling your deep depression and hopelessness.
- It helped you manage your weight.
- It allowed you to indulge on so many foods you otherwise would not have.
- It forced you into a deep spiritual inquiry.
- It was the catalyst for you becoming vulnerable, maybe for the first time.
- It tried to help keep you alive. You were starving, remember?
- If you were ever suicidal (most addicts have had the thoughts), bulimia distracted you enough to never act on it.
- It was your shield when you were too weak, sensitive, and vulnerable for what the world was throwing at you.

Write down and ponder all the gifts your bulimia has given to you. Then actually thank your bulimia. You may even choose to write a letter to your bulimia, thanking it for everything it has provided. Then create a cathartic ceremony where you burn the letter and symbolically release your bulimia. Its purpose will have been fulfilled.

Treasure Your Recovery

Now start picturing the future—a future where you are free from bulimia and your life is wildly better. That future may be later today, it may be tomorrow, or it may be a month from now. As best you can, simply put yourself in a place of actually being abstinent. Then write down what you see, feel, and think. Who's around you? What accomplishments have you achieved? What dreams are you pursuing? What is your mindset? What has recovery given you? Who have you become? Bask in the wonderful freedom. Write down what you see. The more you can picture this in detail and the more you can treasure it, the more quickly it will manifest. Here are some ideas to get you started:

- Recovery has caused your heart to open wider than you thought possible.
- It has given you a solid foundation for your future.
- It has given you new communication skills to draw from.
- It has provided you with an entirely new set of friends and confidantes.
- It has caused you to deepen your spiritual walk even further.
- You have become much more empathetic in your struggle.
- You are far less judgmental of others still living with addiction.
- You are realizing dreams that were never possible outside of recovery.
- You are mentoring others and changing lives.

You will find that once you sit in the space of deep gratitude, the purpose of your eating disorder and subsequent recovery will begin to materialize. You will actually see where each has served you. You will understand that you are becoming a person you would never have become if you had lived the status quo. You were never one to flat-line life, so of course you took your eating disorder to an extreme. This is who you are. You are an explorer, an adventurer, a rebel. Embrace this part of you, and be thankful for it.

Appreciate Being Spared

I just wanted to end this chapter by highlighting the absolute miracle you are and hopefully bring you to an even deeper level of appreciation. Bulimia can be a killer. And the fact that you are reading his book is proof that you can be grateful it didn't take you out. You might have had a heart attack. You might have crashed your car as you were binging while driving. You might have burst the lining of your stomach and died. You might have been so hopeless after decades of fighting this battle that suicide seemed a relief. But you are still here.

Those are all critical things to be thankful for. But there are dozens of others to consider. Bulimia destroys your mind, body, and soul. It robs you of authentic and abundant living. Be so thankful that bulimia didn't leave you with permanently ruined teeth, a ruptured esophagus, or broken bones. Be grateful that as you recover, your mood swings, your ability to handle stress, your facial swelling, your red eyes, and your feelings of separation will all heal. Be grateful that you are entering into recovery before something really bad happened. Or if something already has, be grateful it wasn't worse. You have likely suffered from much loss through the years of your eating disorder, but you can end the hemorrhaging today. You can start living. You can abandon the risky behaviors and enter into the life you were destined to live. You have been playing Russian roulette. Put down the gun while you still can.

Freedom Exercises

1. Write a thank you letter to your bulimia.
2. Write a scene from your future life in recovery. Include as much detail as possible. Who is there? What do you see? What do you smell? Where do you live? Have you won any awards for your accomplishments? What dreams have you fulfilled?
3. Create a list of all the things that could have happened to you during your active bulimia that didn't. Stand in a deep level of appreciation for all you have been spared.

CHAPTER 12

FREEDOM STRATEGY 10:
HELPING THOSE STILL SUFFERING

*"Be loving towards yourself, then
you will be able to love others, too."*
—Osho

You've worked so hard on your own recovery through the first nine strategies, so helping another overcome her eating disorder may seem like the last thing you are capable of at the moment. But I assure you—stepping outside of yourself to help someone who is even just a few days or weeks behind you can be vital to your recovery.

The last and final of the 12-Steps of Eating Disorders Anonymous is "Having had a spiritual awakening as the result of these steps, we tried to carry this message to others, and to practice these principles in all our affairs." Whether you have worked through the 12-steps or not, this is a great recovery strategy. Reaching out to others who are suffering will help solidify your own healing. I'm not suggesting you mentor or sponsor someone while in your own very early recovery, but you can absolutely walk side-by-side with your sisters for mutual support at any stage of pursuing abstinence. But only if you're ready. First make sure you are committed to your own recovery—you can't give away what you don't have. I love the saying "Beware of the naked man who offers you his shirt." First put on your own shirt of commitment before helping button up another's.

I started reaching out to others after I was about three months purge free. Looking back, I was still so raw and tender, but strong enough to know I wasn't going back to bulimia. I began sharing my struggles and victories, and soon people were asking if I could be in touch with so-and-so's friend who is still struggling or so-and-so's daughter who needs help. This was such a blessing. Being able to stand alongside someone in those early days really helped strengthen my recovery.

Brianna

The following is an email exchange from a gal I supported over the course of a few months during her very early recovery and, frankly, mine. I share so you can see the very typical chain of events and so you can know recovery is possible even when the path is a little wonky. Before we began meeting, Brianna was binging and purging most days and couldn't see her way out. She was not in heavy therapy or even attending recovery meetings. She had just decided she was done with bulimia and shared that with someone in a self-development course she was attending. That person was my brother. As you will see below, abstinence is sometimes a two-step-forward-one-step-back process, but eventually you can be free. I changed her name, but the rest is as written.

Hey Brianna,

Great to chat with you. You can do it! And thank you for being part of my continued recovery. It's a gift to help in this small way.

Big hugs,

Lori

Hello Lori,

I have built an identity on being a victim in many ways. It's a default pattern of behavior I am working consciously to change. So far, no binges since we spoke

Brianna

Hey Brianna,

Wow. That's fantastic! You go girl,

Lori

Hello Lori,

I have thought for some time that my bulimia was really about survival and the book you recommended gives a new perspective into that theory. I've now had 5 days of success with not binging! On the weekend I struggled with over-eating. I have now made an agreement with my roommates to stick to a meal plan, as that seems to help a lot.

B xo

Hey Brianna,

That's fantastic! No purge though? The process seems to go something like:

Purging stops.

We continue to over eat occasionally, but refuse to purge. This is the miracle.

There may be a few pounds of weight gain and we freak out.
We struggle acutely with body image issues.
These finally subside as balance returns and we get on with life. ☺
So you are exactly perfectly where you need to be. It is a journey. I'm only 10 months purge free and I've followed the above to a T. You're doing it. So proud of you. Keep it up!
Xo L

———————

Hello Lori,
10 months purge free? Wow! Do you still get urges? No purge last week. I'm following my meal plan. Being on it may be inconvenient, but it's far more inconvenient to be stuffing myself and then throwing up all the time.
Bri

———————

Bri,
You go, girl. Yes, the urges start to subside. And the ability to resist increases. I'll look forward to your stellar report on Monday.
Lori

———————

Hello Lori,
I had a set back today. I had a mini binge purge episode with two cupcakes and some plantain chips. Frustrating. Back to the meal plan tomorrow. I remind myself that my binge thoughts are "neurological junk," but today my binge voice is telling me at the same time that it's ok.
Soldiering on tomorrow.
XO

———————

Hey Brianna,
Thanks for the e. Sorry to hear about the little blip. You have done incredibly well for a number of weeks and that's FANTASTIC! I'm not even sure what to say that will help, except you had a really great run of

abstinence and don't beat yourself up. Just get back on the horse quickly. Keep it up. You're doing so so well.

Lori

Hello Lori,

It has been a challenging week. I did have one binge purge episode. And have overeaten for a few days now. It's frustrating because I know better, but when the urge comes up I keep following it, like an obedient dog. Autopilot. Argh.

B

Bri,

Omg, I understand the obedient dog/autopilot program. Yup. That's bulimia for you. But we are taking back control! You've got this.

Love Lori

Hello Lori!

Things have been looking up for me. I have simply decided to be bulimia free. It has been about 12 days now. It's just easy now that I've made up my mind not to continue sitting in my lower brain's habitual patterns. I can't thank you enough for your support.

B xo

Bri,

Holy s***! Yay. This made my day. I'm really proud of you. I know how hard it can be, but somehow once you make the decision to stop, it's so much easier! Other things fill the space where the constant obsessions once lived. Can you believe yourself? What a strong courageous woman you are! Do you see it?

Lori

The above dialogue was between two women who at one point could not string two days together bulimia free. I hope seeing the struggle, the commitment, the slips, the emotion, and the process in black and white gives you license to go easy on yourself while also taking your recovery journey super seriously. Brianna took the time to meet with me in person during this stage of her journey, which was no easy feat. She lived a sky-train ride, a bus ride, and short walk away. She played full out and got her just reward—her life back. I hope, sweet sister, you are ready to play full out. You are worth nothing less.

As you begin attending meetings and reaching out in your recovery journey, there will be opportunities to help others. Even if you feel incapable of making a difference for anyone as you are still struggling so much with your own recovery, try not to shy away from walking with others. Power comes in numbers. Healing comes in community. Relief comes in relationships.

Sharing Your Story

I promise there will be many chances for you to give back and to help those still suffering. After the first few years of abstinence, my sharing went from one-on-one, private affairs to radically public ones. I was sharing my story from the stage, on podcasts, on the radio, and even through this book—all terrifying at first because I carried so much shame. But the more I shared, the more I was loved. The more I shared, the more connection I felt. The more I shared, the further I stepped into my destiny. Our biggest MESS can be our biggest MESSage, and bulimia was definitely mine.

As you gain more and more freedom from food, begin thinking about how you can give back. You likely won't have to think long and hard about it—the need for your voice is so prevalent. As soon as you start sharing, there will be people who need you. Try pushing through the fears. You won't be consumed. You can set the pace. Do your best to be available for the next right thing, and the Universe will bring you many opportunities to serve. You never know whose life you will save as you step more fully into your own.

You have come so far, and I trust you have worked through these ten strategies diligently. You have more knowledge, wisdom, and empathy than you realize, and these qualities can change the lives of those still suffering. Don't be afraid to give them all away. As you bless others with these parts of yourself, they will come back to you in abundance. Your gifts to others will also exponentially strengthen your own resolve. This is why you are here.

Freedom Exercises

1. Love yourself deeply and with more self care than you thought possible.
2. As you feel ready, begin reaching out to others walking the recovery road. You are much more likely to reach your destiny traveling with others.

CONCLUSION

"It's never too late to be what you might have been."
—T.S. Elliot

You were created for a much higher purpose than struggling with bulimia one moment longer. You know this to be true, and there is a wildly courageous part of you that's becoming willing to quit. Do you sense it? I know it's a scary thought, and your mind will play all sorts of tricks on you to keep you in bondage. Thoughts like, *you'll never get free*, or, *you'll get so fat trying*, or, *no one will support you*, or, *they will all think you're a freak if you fess up*. Trust me. I have had the committee in my head for decades. But you can speak back. You can begin to regain your sanity by refuting the lies. You WILL get free. You WON'T get fat trying. People WILL support you. They will LOVE you when you fess up. These are truth statements. Write them on your heart. Repeat them in your mind. Over and over until they stick.

In this short book, you've hopefully begun to understand the physiology and the psychology of your eating disorder. These are real things you're combating. It's not necessarily as simple as just stopping the binge/purge cycle, although it can be. But remember, there are often very valid and deeply ingrained reasons for your bulimia, so be kind to yourself. And now that you know some of the reasons, you can start to reconcile them so you can heal.

We've looked at factors such as behavioral and substance addictions, pain avoidance, starvation as a precursor to binging, and millennia of survival instincts. We've touched on the different types of emotional eating and ways to get those legitimate needs met without using food. We've explored the various steps along the road to recovery. As you begin to make changes supportive of your healing, you will get better. The energy in your home will be cleaner. The energy within you will be freer. The energy you attract will be more positive and powerful. As you heal, you will also be a catalyst for change in the lives of those around you. Most humans are addicted to something and are held back from reaching their full potential. As you gain strength, you will be able to reach over and pull them to peace as well. You will be the example. You will shine light on the path to their best and highest self as you step into yours. You will also begin to make peace with food and your body. This might be a long and laborious process. But you now have the tools. You can combat your negative thinking and embrace every part of you, even the wobbly bits. They are just as lovely as the fit bits. You are a beautiful human exactly as you are.

You've also learned how to properly feed your body so you can shake yourself out of starvation mode. As a bulimic, you are wildly creative with your food. Imagine using that creativity for good? Green smoothies, lean proteins, healthy fats and oils. There are so many fantastic food choices that will support your body and your recovery. Explore this arena. Make friends with your favorite Whole Foods and Trader Joe's. Leave the DQs and KFCs behind. Also begin to love your body through movement. Pick your favorite exercise, and get at it with healthy moderation. It will help exponentially.

There are many other ideas, tools, and techniques in this book to draw from, but I encourage you first and foremost to reach out for help. Please don't do this alone. Draw from the list you made in Freedom Strategy 1 and from the resources listed at the back of this book. Choose whomever and whichever speaks to you the most, and reach out. I am also here to help. I've been where you are and know the way out. The main thing is to get the support you feel most comfortable with. I've never heard of anyone recovering from bulimia alone.

My wish for you, dear reader, is that you find peace, happiness, and freedom. Peace with food, with your body, and with your soul. Happiness at your vocation, through your adventures, and in your relationships. Freedom in your mind, for your future and at this very moment. None of these things are possible while you're still in bondage to bulimia. The only way to access them permanently is to dismantle your eating disorder.

As you recover, you'll uncover so much about yourself, others, and the world that you were previously blind too. Your access to the spirit realm will increase. Your desire for adventure will grow. You will feel balanced. Your relationships will deepen. Your fears will subside. You will discover your inner strength and victorious nature. You will have an abundance of energy and joy. Bottom line, you will be out of the muck and mire that once held you down. You will grow wings and soar to places you could never have imagined within the confines of your bulimia. I'm so blessed to have been part of this piece of your journey and would love to connect as you walk into full freedom and beyond.

Are you ready to quit bulimia and upgrade your life?

FURTHER READING

Books

Goodbye Ed, Hello Me: Recover from Your Eating Disorder and Fall in Love with Your Life by Jenni Schaaefer

Taming the Feast Beast: How to Recognize the Voice of Fatness and End Your Struggle with Food Forever by Jack Trimpey, L.C.S.W., and Lois Trimpey, M.Ed.

Rational Recovery: The New Cure for Substance Addiction by Jack Trimpey

Brain Over Binge: Why I was Bulimic, Why Conventional Therapy Didn't Work, and How I Recovered for Good by Kathryn Hansen

The Emotional Eater's Repair Manual: A Practical Mind-Body-Spirit Guide for Putting an End to Overeating and Dieting by Julie M. Simon

Healing Your Hungry Heart: Recovering from Your Eating Disorder by Joanna Poppink, MFT

Recovery 2.0: Move Beyond Addiction and Upgrade Your Life by Tommy Rosen

Constant Craving: What Your Food Cravings Mean and How to Overcome Them by Doreen Virtue

Websites

Rather than Rehab Recovery Coaching http://ratherthanrehab.com/

Eating Disorders Anonymous (EDA) http://eatingdisordersanonymous.org/

Overeaters Anonymous (OA) https://oa.org/

National Eating Disorders Association (NEDA) https://www.nationaleatingdisorders.org/

ACKNOWLEDGEMENTS

This book has been in my bones since 1995 when I returned home from a five-month lock down, at the Remuda Ranch Eating Disorder Treatment Center. While I didn't release my eating disorder until 18 years later, the work I did at Remuda Ranch set the foundation for recovery. I'm grateful for the caring team of nurses, doctors, and therapists who taught me that my eating disorder could be the catalyst for my soul's renewal as well as the impetus for healing my family. I acknowledge the brave souls there who were also willing to face their shadow sides, speak their truths, and commit to a different way of living.

When I returned to Vancouver after Remuda, Lois M and Jenny G were my faithful recovery sponsors. They each witnessed and supported me as I worked through the 12-steps more times than I care to remember. Each woman taught me self-love in her own unique and supportive way. Self-loathing is a common trait among addicts and one that we have to overcome in order to sustain long-term recovery. Thank you, Lois and Jenny!

I had not sought professional help for my eating disorder in the 18 years following Remuda, even though it was a continual battle in my life. Sometimes it was just a nagging annoyance and sometimes it was an all-consuming hindrance to really living. But further treatment, frankly, felt like as waste of time and money—I was that hopeless.

In November 2012, however, I was once again at the place of desperation. I couldn't go on as I was, so I sought help from Cesar Gomez, an eating disorder counselor in Phoenix. I stepped into his cozy office just a few days later, and this Earth angel started working his magic. That first visit was like a dam breaking, and a lifetime of grief gushed out. I thought I was losing my mind. In the brief few months we met before he retired, his exercises and assignments somehow broke a chink in my bulimic armor, and I was able to get well. May 9th, 2013, was my last episode, and I know that bulimia will never again be part of my coping repertoire.

One of Cesar's assignments was that I attend weekly Eating Disorders Anonymous groups. I'm forever grateful for the group of brave women at the Monday night 20th St and Campbell EDA group in Phoenix, where I live most of the year. They were true sisters and we walked into the light together. Brianna, Sara, Rachel, Amy, Diana, Amanda, Crystal, Kim, Kathleen, and Keri, you are soul sisters. Thank you for never judging my shares and for showing nothing but unconditional love, acceptance, and understanding. I hope you have all found your way, fully and completely, out of your disordered eating habits as well.

While I am grateful for EDA and the 12-steps, I am profoundly happy to have found the book *Rational Recovery: The New Cure for Substance Addiction* and the work of Jack Trimpey. His theory effectively turns the 12-step paradigm on its head, and it fully resonated. His work forced the choice—take responsibility and live or don't and likely die. *Rational Recovery* had me take charge, and I'm deeply indebted.

From January 2013, when I first fessed up to my husband, Ken, that bulimia was a current issue and not just a part of my past, he has been nothing but supportive. He truly understands that all humans use things outside of themselves to ease their pain. We have put coping skills firmly in place until the pain of staying the same becomes greater than the pain of changing. He loved me through the change, and I'm forever grateful for his unconditional love and support.

I'm grateful to my writing coach and developmental editor, Dr. Angela Lauria, founder of *The Author Incubator*. She helped me create order out of a jumble of research, ideas, personal stories, and case studies. Beyond her writing mentoring, Angela also helped me see the value I can bring to the multitudes still suffering and encouraged me to step out in a bigger way to help.

Thank you as well to my amazing editor, Cynthia Kane. Prolific author in her own right, she helped this manuscript shine a little brighter so it can be more effective in helping those seeking freedom. She also caught mistakes I was just too close to the words to see. Cynthia was a treasure to work with, and I'm grateful for her love, knowledge, and expertise.

Lastly, a heartfelt thank you to the Morgan James Publishing team, especially David Hancock, CEO & Founder, for believing in me and my message. To my Author Relations Manager, Margo Toulouse, thanks for making the process seamless and easy. Many thanks to everyone else, especially Jim Howard, Bethany Marshall, and Nickcole Watkins. You all rock.

While I wasn't able to write this book all those years ago (I couldn't effectively lead someone to freedom when I was still in shackles myself) I am ready to bring it to you now. The journey was long and arduous, but nothing has been wasted, and sharing these strategies is my service to you—Freedom Strategy 10, in action. I acknowledge you, dear sister. You are on a glorious adventure deep into your soul. You are on a path to awakening. You are becoming free. This is who you are. It might feel hopeless in this moment, but I promise you, it gets better.

You've got this.

ABOUT THE AUTHOR

 Lori firmly believes that your biggest MESS can become your biggest MESSage and bulimia was definitely hers. Lori's dream is to help as many people as possible escape their private prisons of bulimia and embrace full freedom with food and their bodies.

As a three-time bestselling author and workshop creator, she's been privileged to share her ideas in front of businesses, conferences, and spiritual gatherings as well as through podcasts, radio, and TV interviews. Her *Safe Souls* chapter in Jack Canfield's bestselling book *The Soul of Success, Vol. 1* won the Editor's Choice Award. Her book *Safe Souls: Transforming Relationships and Businesses Through the Power of Kind, Clean and Clear Communication* is also an Amazon bestseller. *Rather than Rehab*'s eBook format quickly rose to being a #1 international bestseller as well.

When she's not creating or writing, you can find Lori hiking the trails near her homes in Vancouver and Phoenix or completing higher altitude treks such as Kilimanjaro, Mt. Kenya, Everest Base Camp, and the Salkantay/Inca Trails in the Andes. She supports NGOs that advance prosperity and healing in the developing countries she explores. Lori also loves yoga, reading, skiing, motor-biking, contemporary architecture, horses, and snuggling with her husband and two rescue dogs, Milo and Tessa.

Website: ratherthanrehab.com
Email: lori@lorilosch.com
Facebook: facebook.com/lorilosch
Twitter: @lorilosch

THANK YOU

Congratulations on taking the time to dig into your recovery and your life. I hope you've done some of the action suggestions and are subsequently feeling stronger, more hopeful, and less alone.

To help you on your way to full freedom from bulimia, I'd like to offer you:

- **A free Rather than Rehab Recovery Checklist**. To redeem this gift, please go to www.ratherthanrehab.com/contact and write Recovery Checklist in the subject line.
- **A free 30-minute coaching session**. To redeem this gift, please go to www.ratherthanrehab.com, click on the Free 30-Min Coaching Call button at the bottom of the page, and fill in the short application form. I will be in touch with you within 48 hours to set up an appointment.

Morgan James
Speakers Group

We connect Morgan James published authors with live and online events and audiences whom will benefit from their expertise.

 Morgan James makes all of our titles available
through the Library for All Charity Organization.

www.LibraryForAll.org

CPSIA information can be obtained
at www.ICGtesting.com
Printed in the USA
LVOW12s2131261217
560834LV00007B/1462/P